Celti
an
Glastonbury Zodiac

Mary Caine

CAPALL BANN PUBLISHING

Celtic Saints and the Glastonbury Zodiac

©1998 Mary Caine

ISBN 1 86163 0220

Published by:

        Capall Bann Publishing
        Freshfields
        Chieveley
        Berks
        RG20 8TF

Other works by the same author

The Glastonbury Zodiac. 287pp
The Glastonbury Giants. 29pp
(shortened version of the first title)
The Kingston Zodiac. 36pp
The Tragic Life of Lady Pamela Fitzgerald. 16pp
Video of the Glastonbury Zodiac. 50mins

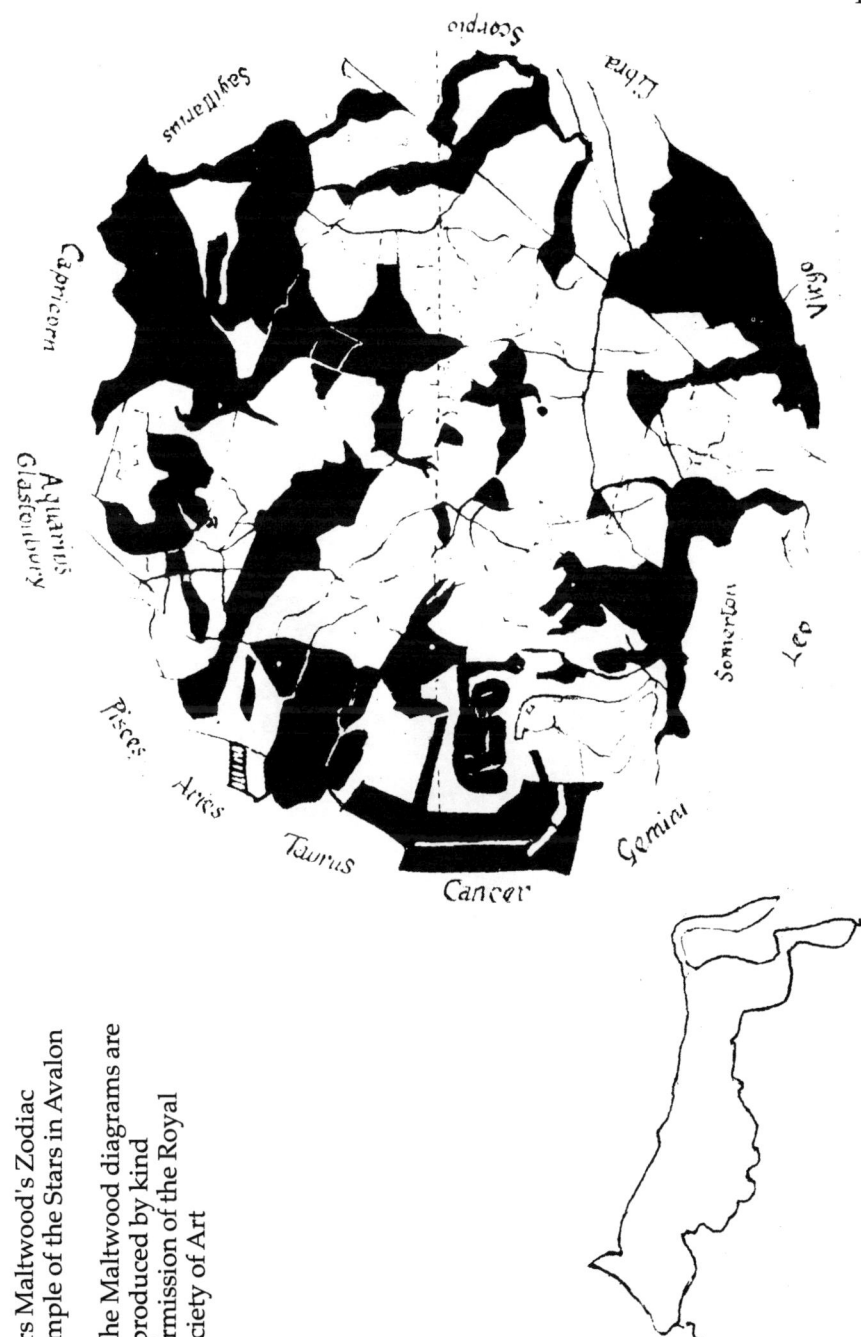

Mrs Maltwood's Zodiac
Temple of the Stars in Avalon

- The Maltwood diagrams are
reproduced by kind
permission of the Royal
Society of Art

Merlin
Arthur
Mordred
Guinevere and Morgan le Faye
Perceval le Gallois
Grail Castle
The Fisher King
Gawain Ector Solomon's Ship
Galahad
Perceval
Lancelot

Mary Caine's suggested alterations of Scorpio, Libra and additions of a second Twin & Draco. See also air photo of Christ-figure in Gemini

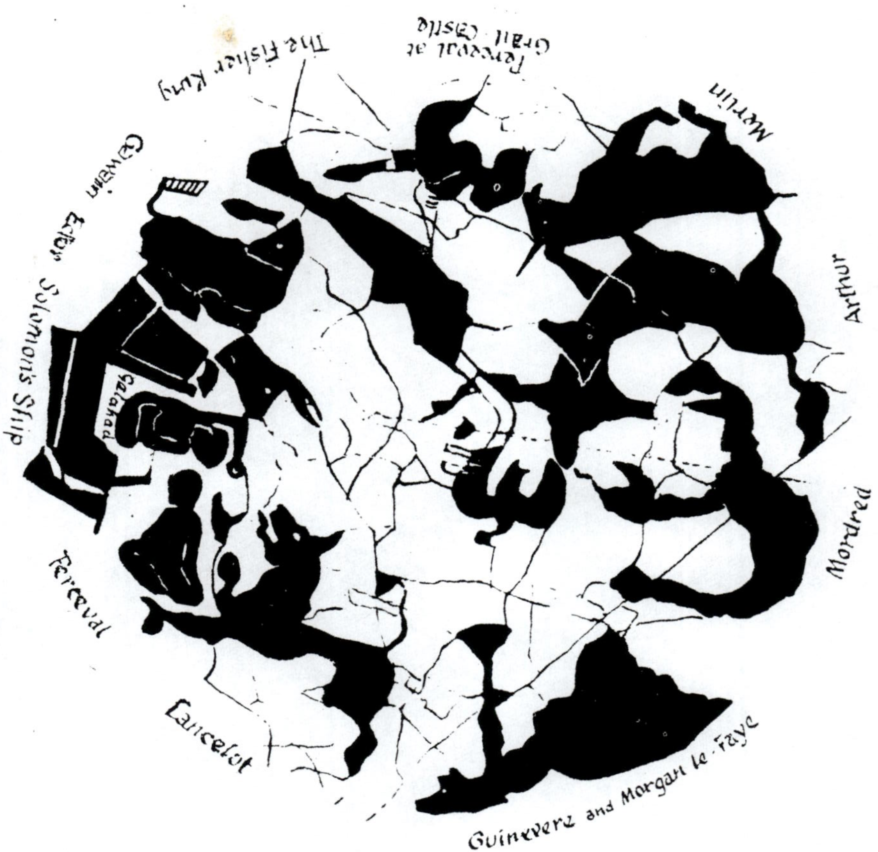

"Girt Dog of Langport"

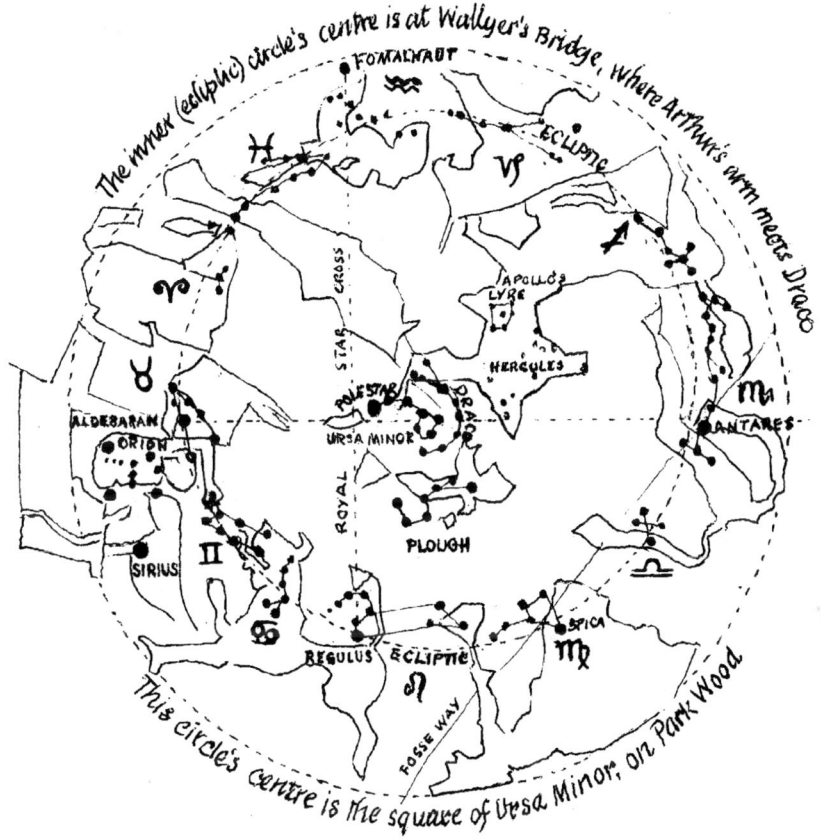

How the Zodiac constellations fit over their earthly effigies when the planisphere is reversed onto the map to scale. The heavens are mirrored on the earth. "As above, so below".
Note the Royal Star Cross. These stars were compass points (due East-West, North-South) about 2700 BC.

4

CONTENTS

CHAPTER 1
Brief outline of the Glastonbury Zodiac   6
CHAPTER 2
Celtic Saints and the Glastonbury Zodiac   18
Joseph of Arimathea   24
Melkin's Prophecy   28
St Ilid   31
St Collen   37
St Patrick   41
St Beon   43
St Brigit   44
CHAPTER 3
St David   51
St Padarn   53
St Nunn   55
St Carantoc   56
CHAPTER 4
The Grail-stone of Parzival   60
St Cadvan   65
St Petroc   66
CHAPTER 5
The Holy Boy   73
St Budoc   73
St Decuman   74
St Kentigern or Mungo   75
St Melor   77
St Keneth   80
St Ffili   82
St Eval   83
St Issui   85
St Sulien   87
St Mabyn   87
CHAPTER 6
St Maternus   97
St Madron   97
St Gengulf or Winwaloe   97
Little St Hugh   98
St Rioche   101

St Roch   102
St Roche of Montpellier   103
StWillow   105
St Huail   106
St Hywel   107
St Kenelm   108
St Helier   110
St Clement   111
St Kea Colodoc   114
St Germanus   117
St Gwynnlyw & St Tathan   120
St Cadoc   121
St Edeyrn   126
CHAPTER 7
St Keyne   130
The 3 Eves of Evesham   134
St Ursula   136
St Dunstan   140
St Blaise   144
Index   148

ILLUSTRATIONS

Diagrams of the Glastonbury Zodiac   1,2,3
Glastonbury Tor   6
Gemini's Three Bars of Light   8
Gemini, Messianic Effigy   10
The Doorty Cross   17
Joseph of Arimathea landing on the rocks of Albion   26
Glastonbury Abbey   27
Bride's Corn Dolly   45
Brigantia   50
Annunciation   55
Two Celtic Saints   72
The God Esus   86
St Kenelm's Tympanun   108
Saint, 8th Century   113
Cernunnos   127
St Edeyrn   129
The Triple Goddess   133
Scorpio   141
St Blaise, painting in Kingston Parish Church   146

Glastonbury Tor

CHAPTER 1

The Glastonbury Zodiac: Arthur's Round Table

As some knowledge of this great Earth-Zodiac is needed in order to recognise its elements as they appear in the saintly lives recounted in this book, I must briefly describe it for those unfamiliar with Britain's most ancient Royal Secret, which was it seems passed down from Celtic kings to their sons. As most of these saints were of royal descent it should be no surprise to find evidence in their legends that they knew of it, and that its teachings were incorporated into Celtic Christianity.

Discovered about 1925 by Katharine Maltwood, sculptor and Fellow of the Royal Society of Arts, the twelve signs lie in a circle ten miles across, contoured by hills, outlined by roads, paths and waterways, and guarded by a great hound at the western approach from the Severn. The river Parret draws his underside from his nose at Athelney to his hind leg at Langport (five miles). The signs are in correct Zodiac order, but it is a mirror image, as if the stars were reflected on this favoured piece of earth in Avalon; and when the planisphere is superimposed upon the map to scale the Zodiac stars fit over their earthy signs.

The effigies are well-proportioned to each other, several being three miles across. The two Piscean fish match in size, as do the two birds of Aquarius and Libra and the two Geminian Twins: all effigies dovetail towards the circle's centre; all heads save one face west. Can all this be arranged by blind chance?

A further piece of design is the "Family Trinity" in an equilateral triangle across the circle, with Sagittarius as the sun-god, Virgo as Earth-Mother and Gemini as their divine Son. This is the creative Trinity of the oldest religious systems— but the Christian version appears also, with a dove replacing Libra's Scales, and flying to fertilise Virgo's Earth-Goddess from Sagittarius's head. As the "Word" this dove often appears in Christian pictures of the Annunciation. The Dove was a sacred messenger from the gods in earlier cults and as the Awen (White-Wings) were signed by the broad arrow or Three Bars of Light by the Druids; a sign still used on Government property and on hill-top trig-points (most suitably) to this day. We shall see these three bars of light descending on babes destined for sanctity in more than one saint's legend.

They are implied in our Zodiac, converging above Gemini's head to a point on the Libran Dove's wing, if we extend the masts of the ship in which he sails. Bisect the angle they make and this resultant third bar pierces the head, ear, heart and mouth of the foetal figure, and down through his groin. This pregnant picture implies much, for here is the timeless Son of the Sun-God and Mother Earth — Man himself — half animal, half-divine, his divided nature at war with itself, his head bent in self-examination. He is Evolution's latest product as it feels its way through myriad forms toward ever-growing consciousness.

  Can he hear with his ear and feel with his heart and relay through his mouth the Word so subtly piercing him from High? He sits in his ship like many sun-gods of myth — Horus, Moses, Theseus — cast at birth to the mercy of the waves. All the Zodiac animals look towards him in hope — fishes, reptiles, birds, mammals — all of them evolutionary steps, growing ever more complex through the aeons.

8

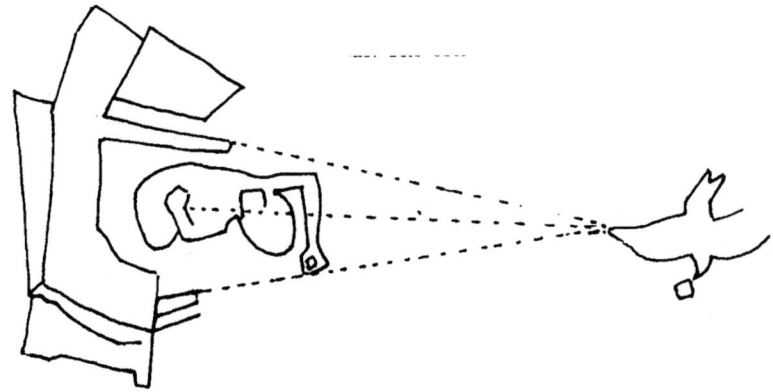

The Three bars of Light

All life began in sun–warmed seas. The constellation Argo Navis, the Ark, Cancer's sky-neighbour, here replaces the Crab, and is a vastly superior symbol, being at once moon, womb and tomb for its foetal occupant, who emphasises that Cancer ruled by the moon is the Zodiac's maternal sign. As this lunar-crescent ship is man-made, being cut in straight drainage-dykes or "rhynes", it looks as if it were consciously designed by men who understood the Zodiac's message. At once draining the marsh for ploughing, they also recorded their arrival by ship in search of the metals for which western Britain was well-known; Mendip lead, Welsh gold, tin from Dartmoor and Cornwall.

Were they Phoenicians, who are known to have mined here, and are even thought by some to have founded a ruling line by intermarrying with the aboriginals? Or were they Sumerian as Mrs Maltwood claimed, colonising us way back in 2700 BC? Either way, eastern king–names and place-names occur in early Britain, particularly but not exclusively in the west. Kings like Belinus, Cunobelinus, Cassibelaunus, Duke Solomon of Cornwall, or Alfred's adviser Asser of the Welsh royal family, (to mention but a few), show indebtedness to Middle-Eastern colonists, who in turn took their names from the sun-god Bel or Baal, Assyrian Asser, or Jewish Solomon (Sol the sun). Cader Idris is a name as Syrian as it is Welsh. Prefixes like Tal and Bedd occur both in Wales and Palestine, and have the same meaning. (Tal in both means tall, raised-up; Bedd or Beth in both is a resting-place or grave). Many hills and mountains in the Celtic West still bear the sacred prefix Bel, Bal or Bally.

These merchants may have brought the Druids to Britain and Ireland as missionaries, following trade. They were famed star-gazers, astrologers, law-givers; they taught the immortality of the soul, and its self-perfection through reincarnation. They inquired diligently into the causes of natural phenomena, and their schools in Britain were resorted to by the noblest youth of Gaul, as Caesar states. There is a tradition that Pythagoras himself was initiated in a grove of Marseilles. Lucan gives their Trinity as Teutates, Taranis and Esus, apparently by his time an all-male one — but Robert Graves suspects that Taranis was originally the Earth-Mother Black Annis, who still survives in remote parts of our islands. British Anna — Britannia.

In Phoenician Carthage she was Tanit, her son, Eshmun or Iesu-munu, around 500 BC. There were Phoenician kings named Eshmunazar and Eshmun-Asser. The astrologer Teucros of Babylon, born in 90BC, says of Virgo — "The Virgin holds a boy in her arms; his name is Ysu". Eshmun, Iesus, Esus... It would seem that Jesus was named from non-Jewish but contingent religions, and that such a name implied membership of a universal Trinity— a son of God and Mother Earth who must suffer and die to lead his people upward.

Phoenicians celebrated Eshmun's birth, mourned his death and rejoiced at his resurrection with great annual rites and public displays of ecstasy or grief that were much too orgiastic for our northern taste; on their Good Friday men cut themselves and ran about dripping with blood, women tore their hair out and ripped their clothes in the streets, weeping and howling.

Roman-Celtic carvings of Esus have been found, one beneath the nave of Notre Dame in Paris, see page 86. He is young, and cuts a branch from a willow — a tree that both heals and mourns, and will reappear in these pages. Esus is both healer and woodcutter — Jesus was both healer and carpenter.

On one carving two birds and a bull's head nest in the tree — Taurus and the two birds of our Zodiac? On another Esus holds his axe-wielding arm above his head at right-angles, reminiscent of our Gemini figure.

Years ago when I first began to study the Maltwood Temple of the Stars I was totally unaware of the prevalence of pre-Christian "Christs" in the ancient religions of the east. So I was amazed when contemplating the air-photo of Gemini in her "Aerial Supplement" (now out of print) when another figure emerged from within the foetal Babe — beautiful, bearded and undoubtedly messianic; the head is finely drawn, forehead and nose emphasised by the rampart of a British Camp on Dundon Hill. (Bronze Age? Bronze rings were found there). His hair and beard are woods, his eye a slightly sunken watershed, now overgrown, which might once have sparkled, as did the eyes of perhaps all the effigies, in early days. Taurus' eye was a pond in Trays Farm until recently.

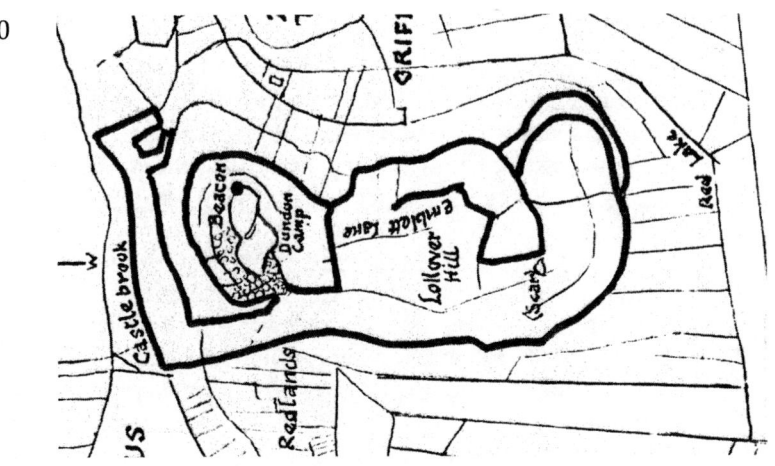

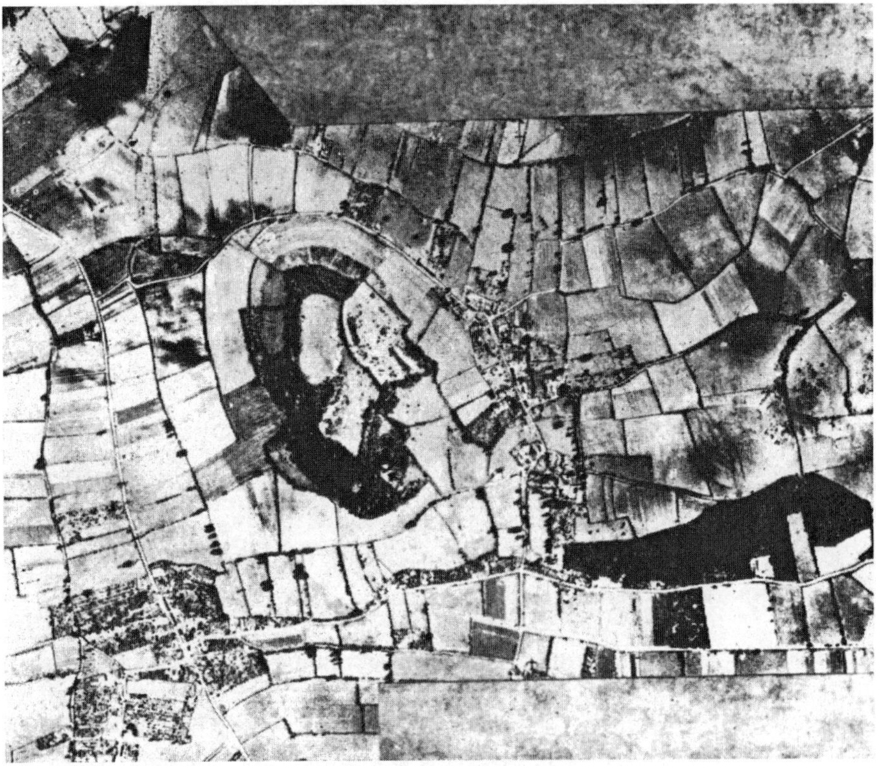

The Messianic figure contained within Mrs Maltwood's Gemini child

Here was the young and dying god-man of the ancient Mysteries; the long-desired fulfilment of the Babe in Evolution's womb-boat. A suffering figure, his hands are tied at the wrists above his head by long field-strips like thongs, as if flagellated at a pole, or crucified on a tree–trunk — a practice in ancient times.

Is this figure natural, or partly man-made? The two hills that model him are obviously natural, the rampart tracing his face obviously man-made. But this too may follow a natural contour, as the most economical in effort. Did Mother Nature model her Son? She certainly began this work, for seen from Walton Hill on the Ram these two hills look very like a giant baby half-buried in the earth.

There are other man-made refinements; a tumulus-beacon on top of his head, the place of the pineal gland, seat of illumination in the Mysteries; strip-lynchets define his rib-cage; old field-strips draw his ribs; a "wound" of red marl persists on his groin, and is pierced by the central ray from the Dove, reminding us of the Maimed King of Avalon's Grail Castle, and of the Lance of Longinus. The very name Lollover Hill (his body) seems to recognise the lolling head of the god; Dundon, we are told, means Fort of Wisdom, Inspiration.

Not the least of Katharine Maltwood's startling claims is that this Zodiac is the original Round Table of Arthur in Avalon; he, with his chief knights, Merlin and Guinevere being still seated round it as the signs of the Zodiac and seasons of the year.

Much evidence supports her. The 13th century MS, La Queste del San Graal, says for instance - "The Round Table was constructed, not without great significance on the advice of Merlin, and was meant to signify the round world, and the round canopy of the planets, where are to be seen the stars and many other things." So it was no mere banqueting-board. A passage in Morte D'Arthur describes it as big enough to feed four thousand people and 150 bulls, some black, some white, some spotted. This must refer to a large tract of land; the bulls we are told are the knights, of various shades of virtue. Obviously among the "many other things" this table signified was astrology's ancient system of psychology, a potent tool in the quest for self-knowledge. The knights in questing the Grail were in search of their own signs - *themselves*. "Man, Know Thyself", was an axiom of the Mysteries. "As above, So Below", was another. The stars mirrored on the earth...

How did Mrs. Maltwood come to make this momentous discovery? She had been asked by Dents the publishers to read the "High History of the Holy Grail"- a translation by Sebastian Evans of a Norman-French MS usually known as "Perlesvaus" written c.1220 at Glastonbury Abbey. They required her to draw a map of the itinerary of the Grail-questing knights round the Vale of Avalon; this she did in 1929. It was while perusing the map of the area that the great lion of Somerton leapt out at her with a roar, his underside accurately drawn by the River Cary. She remembered that more than one knight had encountered a lion in their adventures, and when she next saw the Giant Babe of Gemini clearly contoured by Dundon and Lollover Hills and recalled their fights with giants, she took the map to a friend who happened to be interested in astrology, and who suggested that these figures from their relative positions might be part of a Zodiac. Before long they had traced the rest of the circle's figures on the map, using roads, paths and waterways, and the numinous realization dawned that the Round Table and Grail legends arose from this vastly more ancient Zodiac, and indeed preserved the memory of it in code. Mediaeval monks recorded that Avalon had long been haunted by a Lion and a Giant — the very effigies she had first seen on the map. - The Tor is traditionally haunted by a goat (Capricorn) and Wearyall Hill by a great salmon, naming its eastern end Fisher's Hill. (Pisces).

Sebastion Evans in his preface to his translation of Perlesvaus claims the book as the first Grail Romance from which several others derived in quick succession in the 13th century in France. Scholars have disputed its priority since, but it seems only common-sense that the first Grail-Romance should emanate from Glastonbury. Arthurian legend was known at that time as "Le Matiere de Bretagne", after all. It is the only one that shows detailed knowledge of the local landscape, moreover; so much so that K.Maltwood was able to draw her itinerary from its directions and descriptions. And at the end of Perlesvaus the author (who remains anonymous) tells us that it was the first to be written, being taken from a book in Glastonbury Abbey "so ancient that only with great pains may one make out the letter".

The four main knights whose adventures are related in Perlesvaus are fortunately familiar to us all. Mrs Maltwood assigned them to the four seasons of the Zodiac year; Perceval to the first quarter, succeeding King Pelles as Grail-Keeper after the death of that King of Aquarius' Grail Castle; Gawain to the second or spring quarter as Aries; Lancelot to the third or summer quarter as Leo, and Arthur himself to the fourth quarter as Sagittarius.

So far so good. But there are twelve signs or months to be identified with corresponding knights, and the characters in Perlevaus (excepting these four) are seldom those of Malory's later and far better-known Morte

D'Arthur, the Round Table as we know it. So as few are familiar with Perlesvaus, I have made an amended list, keeping her four chief knights as before, but suggesting better-known figures from Malory whose characters are readily identifiable with the Zodiac signs, instead of those from Perlesvaus which are unkown to the general reader. I suspect in fact that the very obscurity of some of her identifications has been an obstacle to more general understanding and acceptance of her discovery. Hoping thus to clarify the subject, I feel justified by Katharine Maltwood's assertion in her "Glastonbury's Temple of the Stars" that "we know now that all Arthur's knights had their stellar counterparts."

Here is her list from Perlesvaus, with their corresponding Zodiac signs.
1. TAURUS (Earth) who "opened the year with his horns" c2700 BC
   = King Gurgalain.
2. ARIES (Fire) = Gawain, the sun in the 2nd Quarter.
3. PISCES (Water) = The Fisher King.
4. AQUARIUS (Air) = King Pelles, Grail Keeper, succeeded by Perceval. Sun in the1st Quarter.
5. CAPRICORN (Earth) = The King of Castle Mortal.
6. SAGITTARIUS (Fire) = King Arthur. Sun in 4th Quarter.
7. SCORPIO (Water) = The Hermit Calixtus, his soul weighed in the Scales of Death.
8. LIBRA (AIR) = the same Scales. but she thought Libra may also be the Dove.
9. VIRGO (Earth) = The Damsel Dindrain, Perceval's self-sacrificing sister.
10. LEO (Fire) = Lancelot , the summer sun, in the 3rd Quarter of the year.
11. CANCER (Water) = Also Lancelot of the *Lake.*
12. GEMINI (Air) = Lohot, Arthur's son, the western setting sun, the 1st twin. Also Orion. The 2nd Twin, Perceval, is represented by the Griffon on the rudder of Orion's Ship.
13. Canis Minor, the Little Dog's head = The Child, Meliot of Logres.
14. Cetus the Whale = Gohaz of the Castle of the Whale.
15. Draco, the circumpolar dragon = The Black Knight, the Giant Devil.
17. Hydra, the Serpent = Queen Guinevere.
18. The Great Hound of the Parret River = the wife of Marin the Jealous.

But where are such notable characters as Merlin, Tristram, Ector, Mordred or Galahad? Or Morgan le Faye, or the Lady of the Lake? I have given them a place in my amended list. And can it be right to relegate Guinevere, the Round Table's queen, to Hydra's insignificant stars, which are not even a sign of the Zodiac? Surely she should be Virgo, to whom as Earth-Mother all the Zodiac land belongs, and thus takes her place in the Zodiac's Family Trinity of Sagittarius, Virgo and Gemini.

Galahad does not figure at all in Perlesvaus, but as his name is a variant of Lohot Arthur's Geminian son, I have placed him in that sign. For who can the Christlike Galahad derive from, if not the Messianic figure that appears so clearly within the Gemini Babe?

Here is my list.

1. ARIES = Gawain. Arthur's nephew. The first knight to begin the Grail-Quest. Aries is traditionally the Zodiac's first sign. Aries-like he failed to finish his quest.

2. TAURUS = Ector, a knight of substance who faithfully fostered and sheltered the infant Arthur.

3. GEMINI'S 1st twin = Galahad the Christlike knight. Also Meliot of Logres, who dies young. (Logres is traditionally the Zodiac area of Somerset). Also youthful Tristram "The Sad God" who saves the Cornish from bondage.

GEMINI'S 2nd Twin = Percival who follows Galahad his ideal, only catching up with him at last in Solomon's Ship. Percival is Ourselves as we are; Galahad the Man of Evolution's goal.

4. CANCER = Solomon's mystical Ship which sails through Time bearing Man to his goal, the Star-City of Sarras. The Lady of the Lake is also Cancerian.

5. LEO = Lancelot the invincible sun of high summer. Successful in this world, but fails to see the Grail through his too-earthy love for Guinevere. Also King Leodegrance of Camelot, Guinevere's father, who gave the Round Table to Arthur as dowry on her marriage.

6. VIRGO = Guinevere, Queen of the Round Table Zodiac, the Earth Mother. But as a triple Goddess, all women in one, Virgo must also be virginal Dindrain and perhaps Morgan le Faye the Witch.

7. LIBRA = The Dove that flies before the Grail Procession. Also Arthur's spirit escaping from his Sagittarian head as he dies at year's end. A sun-ray enlightening and fertilising Mother Earth at Virgo. The logos or Creation's Word.

8. SCORPIO = Mordred Arthur's nephew-son, the dark enemy who brings down the Round Table, using the scandal of Lancelot and Guinevere to divide the Fellowship. Also perhaps King Lot, Arthur's enemy.

9. SAGITTARIUS = King Arthur. Sagittarius is the House of Higher Mind, the philosopher King. Is he Ahura of the Medes and Persians, who was anciently assigned to Sagittarius?

10. CAPRICORN = Merlin. Capricorn ruled by Saturn, old Father Time, suits hoary Merlin, repository of Druid wisdom. As designer of the Round Table he deserves a place in it. Also perhaps King Bagdemagus – Baghdad Magus?

11. AQUARIUS = King Pelles (several variants of this name) of Grail Castle. Succeeded by Perceval after achieving the Grail.

12. PISCES = King Fisherman, his brother. Sometimes called king Peschour. The maimed king, healed by Galahad. Also perhaps Joseph of Arimathea who landed on Wearyall Hill, founded the Abbey (the old Church), and was reputed ancestor of most Grail-Questing knights.

13. CANIS MINOR = the "brachet" who leaps up to Tristram at the court of his enemy, thus betraying him. As in the Zodiac.

14. CETUS the Whale. Castle of the Whale. A whale swallows Arthur in Layamon's Brut. In Malory Arthur dreams he is, like Sagittarius, upside-down on a wheel with monsters of the deep and serpents, all "taking him by a limb".

15. DRACO. Lancelot as well as Perceval fights a dragon. Arthur dreams of one in the sky. Draco's stars overlay its curving neck when the planisphere is superimposed to scale on the Somerset map. His seven heads are 7 pole-stars to which the earth's axis points successively in its slow circling of nearly 26000 years.

16. HYDRA. If we are to assign any member of Arthur's Court to this insignificant, invisible constellation, (its tiny stars, widely spaced, stretch below the Zodiac belt from Cancer to Libra) I would give it to Morgan le Faye the dark witch who with Morgause, Mordred's mother, were both half-sisters to Arthur. Hydra is a sea-serpent, and the prefix "Mor" means from the sea.

18. The Great Hound is the Questing Beast of Arthurian legend, who runs through the forest pursued by various knights. Also called the Glasting Beast, which seems to identify it with the Glastonbury Giants.

I have spent much time describing Gemini's effigy because I believe that so many Celtic Saints' tales derive from him. Whether they are memories of this astonishing Zodiac figure "baptised" into Christian sainthood, or whether recognisable physical details of him were grafted on to historical saintly characters is hard to tell. Enough to say that Gemini's memory must have helped materially in the transition from Druidism to early Christianity in Britain. Druids seem to have recognised the New Faith as a re-statement of their own. At least there were no martyrs in Britain (except three who suffered at Roman hands, not Druidic); and Geoffrey of Monmouth's History of the Kings of Britain says that Druid flamens became Archbishops in the

Celtic church. Druidic Esus, Phoenician Eshmun or Iesu-munu, the third member of an ancient and more universal Trinity, was not difficult to see as Jesus.

I am also anxious to reinstate Meliot of Logres, whom Mrs Maltwood relegated to the status of the little dog of Canis Minor. Here I believe is an ancient name of the Messianic Gemini figure, self-sacrificing son of the sun, Son of God and Man. Meliot also deserves to sit in Gemini's Siege Perilous, though his name was a fading memory when Arthurian myth was written down. In Perlesvaus, if not the first, at least among the first Arthurian Romances, Perceval had "many a time heard tell of his chivalry and of his great valour". He is killed in the flower of his youth by treachery. By the time Malory wrote Morte D'Arthur, he had multiplied into several knights of similar names - Meliagrance, Melias de L'Isle, (Isle of Britain), Melot de la Roche, etc. etc., few of whose exploits are recalled – sure sign of an ancient god near-forgotten. I believe him to be Amalech or Amalek son of the Phoenician Trinity of Baal and Anahita, brought here by eastern trader-ancestors who became kings in western Britain. The King of Love (Amo- I love, Melek- king). Was he the god of the Amalekites of Canaan, whom the invading Israelites smote hip and thigh? I suspect Amalek was a sun-god, for in Exodus chap.17, Moses makes the sun stand still while Joshua defeats the Amalekites.

It seems this Phoenician "family" Trinity came here in early times, for Howell the Good, king of South Wales c500AD, had for ancestors "Aballach, son of Amalech, son of Belin the Great and Anna". There are other similar old Welsh family trees in Jesus College Oxford.

But Aballach or Avallach is the Maimed and Christlike suffering King of Grail Castle in Arthurian Legend, who as "Evelake" was said to have come from just that area between Egypt and Palestine which was inhabited by the old Amalekites. Intriguing then to find in the Penwith part of Cornwall such place-names as Amalveor (a jagged Tor), Amalwhiddon and Amelebrea; Phoenician tin-mining country. They also traded in Ireland for gold; the sacred word Amal occurs in Irish kings' names.

In the Kingston Zodiac the northern Twin has a remarkably Christlike head drawn by the rivers Mole and Ember near Esher, Surrey. Can it be chance that these rivers were once called the Amele and the Emele? Can Esher remember Celtic Esus? I mention Amale or Amele at this length because I suspect that not only the Meliots, Meleas's and Melwas's of Arthurian legend derive from him but several Celtic saints, Malo, Meleor, and Melor - St Melor of Amesbury being remembered suspiciously near Stonehenge's great sun-clock.

The Doorty Cross
Kilfenora
Co.Clare
Ireland

CHAPTER 2

Celtic Saints and The Glastonbury Zodiac

The mystery of forgotten Celtic saints must intrigue many who read their names on signposts as they cross the Tamar or the Severn, westering into Wales or Cornwall. They proclaim that we are now in foreign parts, despite the ease with which we invaders can sweep into this strange territory across huge new bridges and trunk-roads – no border-posts, no passports – and that we are among a people with a different ethos, one that honours its local saints and remembers its Dark-Age roots. Yet these roots are our own; these saints are our own ancestors, for the Celts once inhabited all Britain. And with so many shining lights, can we really call the Ages they illumined Dark?

"St.Keyne" we read as we speed by – "St Neot", St Mabon". Who were they? Those whose curiosity impels them down narrow winding lanes to these villages will seldom find much to satisfy them locally, alas; too often it is only the name that is remembered today, not the deeds.

Many are documented, but often only in old Welsh, Breton or Latin MSS. languishing in museums and cathedral libraries, still awaiting verbatim translations into English. Baring-Gould, Rees, Doble and other hagiographers have given us excerpts for which we must be grateful, but too often their Christian devotion is a source of frustration to those who want the whole story, for their accounts tend to waver and dry up when they confront anecdotes which they consider too absurd, pagan or derogatory to the saint in question. The more I read "But I will not weary the reader with the obviously fabulous legends of this saint", the more I need to know them. For in these despised fables may lie clues to lost teachings of the Celtic Church, tell-tale traces of Druid beliefs, hints of Arthurian and Zodiacal connections, and of a vast Cosmology at once more in tune with the stars and with Mother Earth than that of its successor and suppresser, the Church of St Augustine.

However, enough of these small fish have filtered through the hagiographers' censoring net to give promise of more still in the sea of untranslated manuscripts. Such as I could catch I now present, hoping that those better equipped than I for such sport will go fishing too. The Celtic Salmon of Wisdom still swims, uncaught, in Severn Sea...

In my many years' research into the Glastonbury Zodiac Celtic saints appeared so often that I began to suspect that they knew of it. Could they have taught its Mysteries, seeing their Christianity as a re-statement of its ancient and universal doctrines? Many of their legends can be construed in this light, and indeed only made sense when interpreted thus. Reading between the lines of these apparently fantastic lives one begins to see not just the credulous superstition of the Dark Age, but traces of a sophisticated code, designed at once to conceal from some and reveal to others teachings and ideas dangerous to express in times of civil and religious oppression.

So I have set down as many of these "fantastic absurdities" as I could gather, and must leave the reader to judge for himself.

> There is a greater secret... known to few –
> The magic wand of Mathonwy which grows in the wood
> With more exuberant fruit, on the bank of the River of Spectres.
> Kynan shall obtain it when he comes to reign.
> Taliesin. 6th century

As so many of the Celtic saints were of royal birth they must have known this Secret, which was astronomical, for Math son of Mathonwy was the great Mathematician who measured Time with his rod. The poem is about a "Proud Celestial Circle" reflected on earth by the spectral Giants, and in danger of flood – which often happened to the Glastonbury Zodiac's western side from the Severn. The tree with its exuberant fruit was the Pole-star Tree of Life whose apples were the stars, a druidic concept made clear by another 6th century poet, Merddin, in his poem "Avallenau" – a title which also shows Avalon's circle as its secret centre of inspiration.

Various estimates put the number of Celtic saints between 400 and 700, all crowded into a brief period of about two centuries, from about 450 to 650AD. How much of this extraordinary burst of spiritual activity was due to political causes? Obviously the end of Roman rule in Britain by about 413 must be an important factor; for until then local rulers were appointed by Roman overlords under the Pax Romana. When they left, the sudden freedom brought chaos. There was no system to bring the whole country under one ruler, and the Celtic habit of dividing tribal territory equally among the kinglet's sons soon meant that there was insufficient land to feed their families. Fratricide was soon inevitable and became endemic; the princeling with the strongest arm took all, assassinating this brothers, marrying whoever would strengthen his claim regardless of the "Table of Affinities", banishing whole tribes in his attempt to keep his little kingdom intact.

Gildas inveighs against this tribal disorder with venom, without making any allowance for its underlying cause. Bede also follows him (being like Gildas a Roman sympathiser); both concluded that all was due to the inherent wickedness of the Britons.

Picts, Scots, Irish and Saxons, once they knew the Romans had departed, made matters worse by renewed forays and invasions which the disunited kinglets were in no position to repel. It was against this background that Celtic Christianity flourished - perhaps even because of it. For monastic settlements were a peaceful answer to the vexed land problem. They were almost always headed by displaced royal princes, and these being related to the local tyrant were able to beg enough land to settle their families; and being unarmed and devoted to peace, prayer, learning and hard agricultural labour, were no threat to their patrons. They could even prove an asset by promising to pray for their patron's victory in battle, by cutting down forest, reclaiming land from the sea-shore by building sea-walls, draining marshes by irrigation and when self-sufficient founding colleges of learning on the old and still-remembered Druidic pattern. Baring-Gould remarks that these saints regarded themselves very much as successors of the old bards, and like the bards were often fearless in cursing their overlords if they were tyrannical, or advising them by omens or visions when disaster threatened. Their monastic devotion to learning was appreciated by their rulers who had little time for it themselves, but basked in the reflected glory of their growing reputation. These settlements, sometimes swelling to two or three thousand souls, were a potent social blessing, absorbing and putting to constructive work – and prayer! – beggars, criminals fleeing from justice, starving widows with their families, runaway slaves and other potentially dissident elements; the wise Druidic custom of sanctuary which they continued must have helped materially to keep local rebellion at bay. There was stern internal discipline, enforced by the princely Father of such monasteries or Bangors. Over the gateway of one was written "If a man will not work, neither shall he eat." But there is much evidence in the old records to show that this discipline was enforced by example from the top downwards; the saintly heads of these monasteries vying with their monks in rigorous self-denial, simple living, fasting, and long immersion in cold water reciting psalms to "subdue the lusts of the flesh."

It solved the problems of homelessness, aimlessness, loneliness in old age, poverty, unemployment, social injustice; uniting all in one huge family under spiritual guidance. One could almost wish them back again today...

It is acknowledged today that vegetable gardens, allotments and small market gardens are far more productive per acre than large farms; the amount of land required from the local chief was thus comparatively small;

often the monastery-head would be granted a piece of marsh or forest hitherto uncultivated, and challenged to make the "desert blossom like the rose." This he did cheerfully and with energy, resulting in further gain for his benefactor.

Emigration to Brittany was another solution to the succession-problem; vast numbers of British monks and their families cut down the forests that nearly covered that sparsely populated country in early centuries, hewing themselves living-space where none had lived before. We are much indebted to their monasteries for the survival of saints' Lives, many of which were destroyed in Britain during the Suppression under Henry VIII, and suffered further destruction by Cromwellian soldiery.

It is a significant fact that the great age of the Celtic saints includes the supposed lifetime of Arthur (c470-540) - though it is still a hotly debated question whether he actually lived at all. But if he did not, at least his reputation did at that time, and both "Arthur" and the saintly upsurge were spiritual and national expressions of freedom from the long Celtic subjugation to Roman power so recently departed. If Arthur had not lived, it would have been necessary to invent him (to paraphrase Voltaire), in order to stiffen the resistance of the country to the piratical invasions from east, west and north that began as soon as Roman protection was withdrawn – and to infuse some sense of national unity.

Perhaps he was indeed "invented", or adopted as a tutelary spirit–guardian, like St George or St Michael later on; if so it would be by Druid sages, who though banished to the country's wilder extremities were still active, and locally powerful. Maelgwyn Gwynedd for instance in "Arthurian times" still had a college of bards at his court in North Wales; Strathclyde, Cornwall and Brittany were Druid refuges. Edinburgh, Wales, Somerset and Cornwall all claim Arthur as their own - a situation which would seem to make him king overall. Yet there is no mention of him in British Gildas' Complaining Book written at the time of Arthur's supposed overlordship; a curious omission, since Gildas mentions several contemporary kinglets including Maelgwyn. He castigates them all unmercifully, painting a woeful picture of immorality and internecine strife, quite the opposite of "Good King Arthur's Golden Days."

Nor does the Anglo-Saxon Chronicle mention this saviour of the Celts; odd in the extreme, if Arthur was indeed their chief opponent. True, this Chronicle was first compiled in Alfred's 9th century and relies much on Bede (born c673 at Jarrow) and on Saxon traditions and pedigrees for its entries of the "Arthurian" period, but Bede himself never mentions Arthur, and the Chronicle entries for his supposed period show continuous Saxon invasions and advances against slowly retreating British forces. Battles there were, but by and large the Angles Saxons and Jutes were winning them, consolidating more and more territory in the south and east. There was a lull in the fighting for about forty years towards the end of Arthur's supposed life, when, perhaps exhausted, both sides seemed to live at peace before the Saxon advances recommenced. This lull has been seized on by protagonists of a historical Arthur as proof of his victorious stand - but at no time in this period (or at any other) were the Saxons permanently made to give ground, far less were they banished.

No; one suspects that Arthur is a composite figure, drawn from more than one historical war-leader and richly overlaid with Druidic sun-myth.

The historical Vortigern may have given him his name, for in Welsh pedigrees this is variously spelt as Gwrtheyrn, Weurtheur, even Uthur. In the legends Uther is Arthur's father: thus there is some cause to identify Arthur with Vortimer (also called Gwethigirn) Vortigorn's heroic son, who is credited with banishing Hengist's Saxons – at least temporarily – from their footing in Kent and driving them overseas. They soon came back with renewed strength. There seems to have been an Arthog of the next generation in the north, who may also have contributed to our composite hero. The "Emperor Arthur" may be an added memory of Magnus Clemens Maximus, a Roman-British soldier of the late 4th century who was proclaimed Emperor of Rome by troops in Britain (like the great Constantine before him) and who actually became Emperor of Rome with the help of British troops, though he only reigned for about nine months before being murdered in 383. However, as he married a Welsh princess and had sons by her he figures large in the old pedigrees, and his victorious campaign on the continent may well account for "Arthur's" wars in Gaul. He is the Prince Macsen of the Mabinogion tales. Some claim Ambrosius Aurelianus, another hero of the period, of Romano-British stock, as the true Arthur; and Arviragus, way back in the time of the Roman invasion, may contribute his name and fame to Arthur's. "Hath our great enemy, Arviragus the car-borne British king, dropped from his battle-car?" sang Juvenal the Roman poet.

But though all these and more may have helped to make the multi-faceted Arthur, to none of them belong the *Round Table and the Grail Quest, the very things by which he still lives in our hearts today.* These, both said to be inaugurated by Merlin, hoary symbol of surviving Druidism, are what give him his spiritual dimension and undying vitality. And these are drawn from pre-Christian Mysteries, evidenced by the great Round Table of Glastonbury's Zodiac, and by Arthur's legendary attempts to descend into the Underworld of Annwn to retrieve the Cauldron of Inspiration and Rebirth – forerunner of the Grail.

"Arthur" in fact seems to have represented an ancient system of values and psychological techniques of self-regeneration, which though the Druid hierarchy had long been crushed by the Romans, still obtained in Welsh courts that kept colleges of bards. This is implied by passages in Taliesin's 6th century poems. Perhaps this is why Arthur cuts such a shabby figure in the Celtic saints' legends. Theological argument must have raged between the new Christians and the older theocrats. But though Arthur is often overcome by the saints' superior magic, the outcome, Celtic Christianity, was a fusion of the two traditions, eventually producing Grail Christianity, the Celtic Church's other-worldly answer to the claims of an all-too-worldly Roman Church.

It would be too insular not to acknowledge the contribution to the Grail legends by Moorish Spain, for Wolfram von Eschenbach's Parzifal claims a Spanish Jew Flegetanis and the Provencal Kyot as its source, and the seven planets listed by the medium Cundrie in her prophecy to Parzifal have frankly Arabic names; but this only reinforces the identity of the universal teachings of the Druidic west and the Arabic-Chaldean east, and strengthens the case for Arthur's Round Table as originally a heavenly or starry one.

Nor should the contribution of the Goidelic Celts of Ireland go unacknowledged. Arthur is a recurring Irish name, and it is the opinion of more than one researcher in these ancient matters that the rich heritage of bardic poetry, myth and song in Wales owes more to its Goidelic Celts than to the more recent Brythons.

Be that as it may, it is worthy of note that our greatest cultural flowerings have always occurred when the Celts after ages of oppression and eclipse have been able to express their racial genius. The age of Arthur and the saints, arising after centuries of Roman rule, is only one case in point. The renaissance of Alfred is another - for Alfred, himself half Celtic, brought his biographer-bishop Asser from Wales to educate his Saxon thanes and re-establish a code of laws which include many from Druidic times. The Age of Chivalry, when Arthurian and Grail legends swept across Europe is yet another, and the renaissance under the Welsh Tudors - especially under Elizabeth who flooded her court with advisers, scholars and poets from Wales and Cornwall.

JOSEPH OF ARIMATHEA, though not a strictly "Celtic" saint, is so important in Glastonbury legend that no book on early saints in Britain should ignore him – especially this one, for his legends hint too strongly at the Zodiac. How strange that he should be remembered as landing on Wearyall Hill, the northern Fish; for Christianity's earliest sign was the Fishes. (One *could* land there in Joseph's time; the remains of a Roman landing-stage has been found at the foot of the hill). How strange that his legend makes him plant his staff there, as if to drive in a calendar-peg to mark the coming of the religion of the new Piscean Age. To emphasis its Christian import, it henceforth budded and bloomed not only at Easter, but miraculously, at Christmas – and still does; they send a sprig to Buckingham Palace each Christmas, to prove it. Strange too that botanists identify it as a mediterranean thorn.

Did Joseph choose Wearyall deliberately, knowing the Zodiac Secret? If he never came, it certainly seems as if the maker of his legend knew it; the coincidence is too apt for mere chance. But there is more. Arviragus, king of the Silurian kingdom on both sides of the Severn, is said to have granted Joseph and his followers 12 Hides of land round Glastonbury to maintain them. 12 Hidden Figures? 12 Animal Hides?

The timing of his coming is highly symbolic; the year 63 is the legendary date. For in 61 the Druids had been driven into Anglesey and massacred by the Romans; the Zodiac lay for two years bereft of its hierarchy, its teachers and guardians. On "the third day" Joseph brought resurrection in the form of the new Faith. Arviragus was thus giving the Zodiac into the new missionaries' care.

Gordon Strachan in his "Christ and the Cosmos" points out that this was an awe-inspiring time in the history of the heavens, being not only the beginning of the new Piscean Age of 2160 years duration, but also the start of a whole new precessional cycle of 26000 years. For in the Precession of the Equinoxes the sun slips backwards on this vast time-scale, so that we are now, some 2000 years later, on the threshold of the Aquarian Age. We count Aries as the first sign of the year, so in this vaster scheme it ends the greater cycle, and the Piscean Age begins it anew. Druids, great astronomers, would have been expecting a new Revelation in this unique moment of Cosmic Time, and there are legends, particularly in Ireland, that they knew prophetically of the birth of Christ.

Joseph, Grail legends say, not only brought the Grail but founded a line of Grail-keepers in Britain through his son; from whom descended Galahad, Lancelot, Perceval and many Grail Questing knights; the family tree is given in Malory and elsewhere. Perhaps the tale that Joseph cast the Grail into Chalice Well (Aquarius on our Zodiac) has a message for our

Aquarian Age? But *did* Joseph come here? Was he Jesus' uncle as legend suggests, and did he bring his Nephew to Britain, not once, but as both boy and man in the "Hidden Years?" The tale gives sound commercial reasons for their coming; Joseph, they say, the rich man of the Gospels, made his wealth as a tin-trader, with Phoenician ships plying between Britain and Palestine – a trade as we know already flourishing in the time of Solomon and Hiram of Tyre. There was ancient lead-mining in the Mendips ("deep stone") some seven miles north of Glastonbury, and they still say fervently at one such centre "As sure as the Lord was at Priddy". (It is a curious coincidence that Priddy's lofty radio mast marks the sacred spot today for miles around, a silver streak descending from heaven to earth).

Solomon's Ship, which appears both in Arthurian legend and in the Zodiac, was no mere trading barque; built to last until the Perfect Knight should come, its cargo was the Ancient Mysteries, "Solomon's wisdom".

Joseph connects all Glastonbury's mysteries together, the Zodiac with the Round Table and Grail-Quest. He also connects the royal families of Britain with the Holy Family of Palestine. The Breton story tells how he rescued the Cornish princess Anna, pregnant and turned out-of-doors by her cruel husband, and took her to the Holy Land, marrying her just in time to his brother Joachim, after which she gave birth to the Virgin Mary - which explains how he became Jesus' great-uncle. The Bretons remember poor Anna better than we do, and still revere their Duchess Anne. As we have already seen, traces of this near-forgotten tale still hide in the leaves of Welsh family trees, where Anna, wife of Beli, is sometimes "consobrina" (cousin), sometimes mother of the Virgin.

Did it all happen in fact? Or does it repeat the great myth of our Zodiac, with Joseph as Taurus caring for the young sun-god of Gemini and his mother Virgo, the old sun-god Beli hiding as usual behind the clouds, invisibly seeding Life and Inspiration on earth? History or myth, we are left pondering. For Myth is eternal because it states the human and divine situation in timeless terms. And as myth has a way of repeating itself in history – we can only wonder, stirred, irrationally, to the roots .....

For, preposterous as this "Matiere de Bretagne" seems at first reading – it *could* have happened; the circumstantial details are wonderfully interwoven. Even an impossible miracle like Joseph's Flowering Thorn obliges at Christmas; crimson algae like blood-clots float in Blood Spring at Chalice Well, where Joseph is said to have cast the Grail-Chalice containing the blood of the Crucified. The Zodiac clock keeps inexorable time; and whether Joseph ever came or not, his myth seems to have left us a sign that the Ancient Mysteries are due to be renewed once more in our dawning Aquarian Age.

JOSEPH OF ARIMATHEA among the rocks of Albion by William Blake at the age of 16
By permission of the National Gallery of Art, Washington

Glastonbury Abbey

MELKIN'S PROPHECY

John of Glastonbury in the late 1300s copied a fascinating fragment from a book, ancient even in his time, which he found in his Abbey, that may be the origin of the legend of Joseph's coming to Britain. Indeed, it may be the literary fount of all Grail legends. Here it is, with all its Zodiacal overtones.

"The Isle of Avalon, eager for the death of pagans, for the burial of them all, adorned before all other places in the world by foretelling spheres of prophecy, forever will be honoured by those who praise the highest. Abbadare, mighty in Saphat, most noble of pagans, with one hundred and four thousand, hath there found rest. Among whom, Joseph from the sea, named from Arimathea, has found perpetual sleep; and he lies in a bifurcate line near the southern angle of an oratory made of wattles above a mighty Virgin, worthy to be adored by the aforementioned spheres, thirteen in number, dwellers in that place. Joseph truly has with him in his sarcophagus two vessels, white and silver, filled with the blood of the prophet Jesus. When his sarcophagus shall be found, whole and entire, it shall be seen in time to come, and shall be open to all the world. From that time forth neither water nor dew from Heaven shall fail the dwellers in that famous isle. For a long time before the Day of Judgement in Josaphat these things will be revealed and declared to the living."

John attributed this book to one Melkin, "a seer of the Britons before Merlin." But Professor Margaret Murray (an authority on all things Egyptian) suggests that this lost "Liber Melkini" was originally written by Melkites, Royalist Coptic monks, before the Arab conquest of Egypt in 641. (See the periodical "Ancient Egypt" 1916.) Impressed by the antique style and Middle-Eastern names, at least she regarded it as genuine and not something that John of Glastonbury had invented to bolster up the Joseph legend. For one thing, John could never have called the Founder of Christianity "the prophet Jesus". Nor in fact would a Coptic monk. For another, Abbadare is latin for Abu Adar, Lord of the heavens in Arabian mythology; the one hundred and four thousand with him is the number in the Greek Gematria for Man, the Mikros Cosmos – a Gnostic concept.

Could John have invented all this? And why should he, even if he could? He might well have said that Arthur was buried here – but he didn't. Abbadare must correspond to Celtic Gwyn ap Nudd, Lord of the

Tor and judge of departed souls whom he shepherded into the Underworld. (St Michael has succeeded to his office.) The words Saphat and Josaphat mean Judgement, and are terms with which Phoenicians would be familiar.

Gwyn ap Nudd was one of the "3 Happy Astronomers of Britain" – so like Abbadare he would be at home among the 13 "foretelling spheres of prophecy, dwellers in that place. " And what could these possibly be but the Zodiac effigies with their guardian dog?

Here, it seems, we have the earliest record not only of Joseph's coming to Britain but of the Zodiac on which he landed. The Liber Melkini must have survived the Abbey's great fire of 1184 (in which so many of its books were burned), for Leland, Henry VIII's antiquary, said he saw it there. Alas, it seems not to have survived the Dissolution soon after.

Margaret Murray, feeling like many scholars that Arimathean Joseph is impossible, suggests another Joseph, a Copt from the celebrated Monastery of Baramus in Upper Egypt, who came with his companions to settle at Glastonbury in the third or fourth century. (There are indications of Coptic-type huts there, and they are known to have settled in Ireland. In fact, early Celtic monasteries seem to derive from this pattern.)

She cites variations on the name Arimathea in Grail Legends, such as Joseph ab Armathy, Abarimacie or Barmacie, which she thinks may originally have been Baramus, a name unfamiliar to copyists, who substituted for it one well-known to them from the Bible. But could she have fallen into the usual scholarly trap of "another man of the same name"?

In this mysterious fragment Joseph has in his sarcophagus two vessels filled with the blood of Jesus. Who is more likely to have (or been reputed to have) such relics, Joseph of Arimathea in whose tomb Jesus was laid, or "another man of similar name" from Egypt 200 or so years later? After all, there was much trade between the middle East and Roman Britain in Jesus' time, in which Joseph of Arimathea may well have taken part, as his legends insist.

Whatever the origin of the Liber Melkini, it shows Gnostic awareness of ancient Avalon in the Middle East, and must have passed through later Arabs hands in translation. How else to account for the "Prophet Jesus"? T N Wilde in his "Glastonbury Legends" (to whom I am deeply indebted for much of the foregoing) suggests that it reached medieval Moorish Spain where Toledo was an astrological centre. From there it passed to the

Cathars and troubadours of southern France and home to British Avalon, its original subject – inspiring the first Grail Romances on its way. It must be the inspiration for Perlesvaus (the High History of the Holy Grail), which betrays intimate knowledge of the Zodiac's "foretelling spheres of prophecy", and the anonymous monkish author at Glastonbury tells us that "this book was never before treated but one single time besides this; and the book that was made before this is so ancient that only with great pains may one make out the letter."

St. ILID, patron of Llanilid, Glamorgan, was the Welsh name for Joseph of Arimathea. Moreover according to the Iolo MSS he came to South Wales before settling in Glastonbury.

In the Genealogy of Iestin ap Gwrgant, an IIth cent. prince of Glamorgan, it is stated that Caradoc (the hero who fought so long against the Roman invasion) had for wife one Eurgen, who sent for St. Ilid "from the land of Israel" to come from Rome with Bran, Caradoc's father, to Britain to instruct her people in Christianity. "He became the principal teacher of the Christian faith to the Welsh and introduced good order into Cor Eurgain which she had established for twelve saints near the church now called Llantwit. This Ilid is called in the lections of his life St Joseph of Arimathea". He afterwards went to Glastonbury "where he died and was buried, and Ina, the king of that country, raised a large church over his grave". (Iolo MSS, p 7).

It goes on to say that Ilid came here with Bran Bendigaid (Blessed) and various other followers. The Achau Saint Prydain (Genealogies of the Saints of Britain) states that "There came with Bran the Blessed from Rome to Britain – Arwistli Hen (Aristobulus the Aged), Ilid, Cundaf (the Chief) Man of Israel, and Maw or Mawan, son of Cundaf". There is some early authority for Aristobulus in Britain; Dorotheus, Bishop of Tyre, 303, and Haleca, Bishop of Augusta, both assert this; he was, they say, the Aristobulus whom St Paul saluted in his Epistle to the Romans, and that he was martyred in Britain. In the Triads he is described as "a man of Italy". Arwistli in Montgomeryshire, at least, remembers him. Was he one of Herod's family? The name recurs there.

If Cundaf is not a separate individual but a description of Ilid, then Mawan may have been Josephes, Joseph's son in the Grail legends.

One of the "Sayings of the Wise" in the Iolo MSS, asks

Hast thou heard the saying of St Ilid
One of the race of Israel?
"There is no madness like extreme anger."

Alas, Baring-Gould dismisses Ilid as "a man of straw", being the creation of late Glamorgan antiquaries who were familiar with the legend of the Holy Grail, most probably through Walter Mapes. (This last was Henry II's archdeacon of Oxford, a great enthusiast for Arthurian legend and ancient British history. Geoffrey of Monmouth acknowledges his debt to a Breton book lent him by Walter Mapes or Map). Baring-Gould also dismisses Bran Bendigaid as a purely mythical intrusion of the ancient British god Bran. That these gods have a way of becoming Christian saints cannot be denied, but I am reluctant to dismiss him so easily.

In one British pedigree he is Caradoc's father, in another the father of Caradoc's wife, the sainted Eurgen; Caradoc's father being Cunobelinus, Shakespeare's Cymbeline.

However, let me give a precis of this shadowy period from the pen of R.W. Morgan, a Welsh parson and classical scholar, in his book "St. Paul in Britain" (1860) who was convinced of Bran's historical existence from mention of him in the Welsh Triads and other annals. From Roman sources like Tacitus and the poet Martial Morgan throws fascinating light on this dark period of British history: a period for which one can search in vain for detailed information in more establishment-orientated books.

He tells how Caradoc, British king and heroic war-leader of Siluria (South Wales), after some forty battles with the invading Romans, was betrayed at York by his cousin Cartismandua, bound while asleep and taken in chains with all his family (including his father Bran) to Rome in AD 51. As the old Triads remember, "It was the most complete incarceration known as to families by the Cesaridae".

Caradoc's famous speech before the Senate saved his life. His reprieve was an extraordinary departure from the usual Roman treatment of defeated generals, who were often beheaded and dismembered, their limbs dragged through the streets to the delight of the cheering populace. Morgan suggests that Claudius must have decided that mercy would soothe the outraged Welsh and help them come to terms with their conquerors, while killing him would only inflame their rebellious spirit further. But even without their leader, they fought on. Tacitus says of them "The race of the Silures was not to be changed by clemency or severity."

Though kept a prisoner for seven years, and forced to swear never to take up arms again, Caradoc and his family were splendidly housed in the Palatium Britannicum, and must have lived among the great, for his daughter Gwladys married the Roman senator Rufus Pudens. This Pudens, says Morgan, was the same Roman officer who appears on a dedication-stone at Chichester as giving the site for a Temple to Neptune and Minerva; obviously before his conversion to Christianity. He must have been in charge of the Roman garrison there and might then have first met Gwladys in Britain. The Roman poet Martial – a friend of Pudens – praised her beauty and her wit, comparing the British princess favourably with the Athenian and Roman ladies of the Imperial Court,

> "Claudia, of azure-painted Britons born,
> What Latian wit and Latian grace adorn".

Morgan says that the emperor Claudius also admired her greatly, and to honour him she changed her name from Gwladys to Claudia on her marriage to Rufus Pudens in AD 53. They were converted to the new Faith, and their house became a resort for early Gentile Christians, much visited by the apostles - among them St Peter and St Paul, no less – for which reason their palace was renamed Hospitium Apostolorum. (St Paul came to Rome in A.D.58.)

The four children of Claudia and Rufus, Timothy, Novatus, Praxedes and Pudentiana, grandchildren of Caradoc, were – Morgan avers – brought up on St Paul's knees, and ministered to him until his martyrdom. The two epistles to Timothy, one of which mentions this family, are to this eldest child.

Of Caradoc 'sons, Lleyn or Linus was made Bishop of Rome by St Paul – a tradition confirmed by various contemporary sources. (Clement of Rome, the third Bishop, actually mentions in an epistle that Linus was Claudia's brother). Caradoc's other sons, Cynan and Cyllinus, returned to Britain.

Persecution began in Rome under Nero in the next generation, and all the sons and daughters of Claudia and Pudens were martyred, among them Pudentiana. Their house at length became the first Gentile church in Rome and was dedicated to her. A 2nd cent. stone tablet, still extant there, reads "In this sacred and most ancient of churches... formerly the house of Sanctus Pudens the senator and the home of the apostles, repose the remains of 3000 martyrs, which Pudentia and Praxedes, virgins of Christ, interred with their own hands."

Timothy, (Morgan cites various sources), was martyred at a great age, but before this he went on a later mission to persuade Lucius, his nephew and tributary king under the Romans at Winchester, to become Christian and to convert all in his domain, at about 130 AD. (Lucius dithered, it seems, for his final conversion had to wait for further missionaries in 170 AD..)

The descendants of Caradoc were among the first Christian martyrs in Rome – our first Celtic saints!

In view of all this, it is easier to credit the Welsh tradition already quoted – that Eurgen, wife of Caradoc (though Morgan calls her his daughter) sent for Bran the Blessed and Ilid or Joseph of Arimathea to come to convert south Wales.

Only after this does the Welsh account allow Joseph to go to Glastonbury, where after founding his wattle church there, he died. Eurgen appears in Welsh annals as our first Christian saint; with their help she founded the monastery of Llanilid.

Some say that the identification of Ilid the "man of Israel" with Joseph of Arimathea was only made after scribes of the 1200s had absorbed the Grail legends. But remembering the ancient prophecy of Melkin at Glastonbury Abbey, it is apparent that his coming was recorded there long before that. And the Rev. Smithett Lewis in his book "St Joseph of Arimathea at Glastonbury" has a possible solution to the identification of the two saints. He points out that the Hebrew word El for God (Elohim, gods) is found in both Egyptian and Babylonian inscriptions as "Ilu". Israel appears as Isra-Ilu. So he suggests that Joseph was perhaps called Joseph Ilu – Joseph the man of God. The Phoenicians with whom he is said to have traded had commerce with both Egypt and Babylon. He notes that near Llanilid there is an ancient house called Tre-Bran.

Needing some confirmation of Morgan's wonderful tale, and amazed that it does not appear in Establishment English histories, I turned to Baring-Gould's "Lives of the Saints" for confirmation by a more generally accepted scholar. I found in his chapter on St Claudia much affirmation, though he doesn't see Linus and Timothy as Caradoc's son and grandson... But has he sufficiently acknowledged St Paul's intimate relationship with Caradoc's family in Rome? Readers must judge for themselves, after investigating the evidence.

Notably in his chapter on St Claudia he is more inclined to believe in Bran's historical existence, saying that although Tacitus doesn't mention him at Caradoc's trial, he may have been taken to Rome later. Morgan's version is that he voluntarily went to Rome as a hostage for his son.

Robert de Borron who about 1190 wrote "Joseph", the first Grail legend to bring the Arimathean party on their was to Britain, must have known something of these ancient records. In fact he seems enchanted with the "Matter of Britain" for the next two parts of his trilogy were designed to deal with Merlin, Arthur, and the Round Table. Only part of his "Merlin" now exists. In his "Joseph" however, Bran (his name slightly changed to Bron) marries Joseph's sister; they have twelve children. Although in this Romance we are left in doubt as to whether Joseph himself actually comes to Britain, he gives the Grail (housed in a portable Ark) in charge of Bran and his son Alain, and the party proceeds to the "Vaux d'Avaron" – which can only be the Vale of Avalon.

On their way the oracle from the Ark tells Bron to catch a single fish to feed them all, and for this achievement he is given the title of the Rich Fisher. Was this the Druidic Salmon of Wisdom that fed several subsequent Celtic saints on the cut-and-come-again principle? If so these Christians were absorbing Celtic Wisdom; a fusion furthered by the marriage of Joseph 's sister to Celtic Bron. But the Divine Fisher of souls has been deified from ancient Chaldea, Arabia and Greece; there are eastern Mysteries as well underlying Bron 's `title, which were perpetuated in the mystical Fisher-King of Arthurian legend. A statue of a Fisher-god was found in a Roman temple at Lydney on Severn – in the Mabinogion the Salmon of Wisdom's own river.

We are also told that while Joseph was imprisoned in Jerusalem by the Jews for affirming the Resurrection from his own sepulchre, Christ Himself gave him secret words of consecration before miraculously freeing him from prison. These secret, sacred words were passed on to Bron and subsequent Grail-bearers in Britain, implying a Divine Authority quite separate from the Roman church of Robert's time. And though the missionaries were extremely devout, even mystical, there was something subversive about their piety. Their Grail was oracular, its directions faithfully obeyed.

Invisible and inaudible to the unworthy, was it not the Vessel of the Holy Spirit – of individual Conscience? It was all frankly heretical to orthodoxy, which insisted on total obedience to its priesthood.

Was Aquitainian Robert de Borron a Cathar? This sect in his time exhibited a purity and simplicity of life which put the pompous and worldly Roman church of his day to shame, and its growing popularity in southern France being seen by that church as a threat, it was being cruelly persecuted, and indeed anihilated. It too had come from the east by transmission through the Bogomils of Bulgaria. Robert was himself a minstrel, and it is significant that he dedicated his poem to a Templar, for they also professed a secret form of Christianity which had learnt much from the East.

Was Robert hinting at the existence of a secret Church that by-passed Rome, agreeable in its simplicity to both the primitive one of Jerusalem and the British Celts: in which Joseph, possessed of Christ 's Secret Words, and not Peter, was the Head?

And how did he hear of these legends of Joseph's coming to Britain with Bran or Bron? As a result of the Saxon invasions, many despairing British minstrels fled to Brittany and the west coast of France, harping sad lays of their country 's history. Eleanor, daughter of the Duke of Aquitaine and later wife of Henry II of England, heard them too at her father 's court in her youth, and like Aquitainian Robert became enamoured of them. It was in her time, and no doubt under her powerful influence, that Arthurian and Grail legends began at last to be written down.

Soon after the appearance of Robert 's "Joseph", Perlesvaus or the High History of the Holy Grail was written at Glastonbury. It continues Robert 's tale, for Arthur 's knight Perceval is there a descendant of Alain, Bron 's son, who with his eleven brothers owned twelve castles in Avalon.

But these must be the effigies of its Zodiac, as can be seen by the character of the adventures within them, and by some of their names, which include the Castle of the Bull, and the Castle of the Whale. It was while reading Perlesvaus that Katharine Maltwood discovered this lost Zodiac, for its geography is often clearly recognisable, the anonymous author at Glastonbury knowing the area well.

Robert de Borron possessed a Secret – a very great Mystery which he says nothing would make him divulge; if forced he would even lie rather than tell it. Centreing round an oracular ark-borne Grail (ostensibly a chalice, though he is strangely vague about its form) he calls it the "Vessel in which Christ made his sacrament". It lies in a hidden sanctuary in Avalon for centuries, kept by twelve guardians until the coming of Perceval, their descendant. *Was he punning on the word Vessel?* For there, in the Zodiac is the Christlike effigy of Gemini fitting in his Cancerian ark, (a vessel which reflects the constellation Argo Navis in the heavens) like an acorn in its cup. The Zodiac can be an oracle, and has been used as one for centuries. Is this Robert's great and heretical Secret? It is difficult to imagine a greater Mystery.

St COLLEN, one of Glastonbury's own early saints (7th century), has several legends that seem to betray a knowledge of the Zodiac. Making a thinly disguised appearance are three of the most important figures, the Zodiac "family" Trinity of Sagittarius, Virgo and Gemini. They must have intrigued early Christians. But first we will see him on the Tor where he had his cell, playing the part of Water-Carrier, aptly enough on the sign of Aquarius.

One day he overheard two rustics outside his cell door speaking with awe of Gwyn ap Nudd, Lord of the Underworld of Annwn, who lived on or within the Tor. St Collen popped his head out and told them not to believe in demons. This slight must have reached Gwyn's ears, for he sent a messenger to invite Collen to meet and feast with him on the Tor. He refused, but each day the invitation was repeated more menacingly until the reluctant saint, seeing the challenge must be met, climbed the steep slope, taking the precaution of bringing some holy water with him – no doubt from Chalice Well.

At the top he saw to his amazement a splendid palace alive with courtiers, bards and lovely ladies ministering to Gwyn, who was seated on a golden throne. After a gracious welcome Collen was offered sumptuous viands but declined them. "Have you ever seen courtiers in more splendid livery, all in red and blue?" asked Gwyn. "Ah", said crusty Collen, "but the red is of hell-fire, and the blue is deathly cold". And without further ado he flung the holy water at the company, whereupon they vanished in a flash, palace and all, leaving him alone on the hill-top with only the wind sighing in the grass.

Gwyn ap Nudd besides being Lord of the Fairies was leader of the Wild Hunt who took dying souls to his Celtic Underworld, a place of Eternal Youth, feasting and joy within the hollow Tor. His father, Nudd, is often equated with Nodens, the Romano-British god whose statue was found in his shrine at Lydney on Severn, and with Irish Nuada and Welsh Lludd, both sun gods. But Morien Morgan claims Nudd as Gwyn's mother, not his father, at an earlier time - Nydd or Neith (like Egyptian Nut), goddess of Fate, Night, Death and Rebirth. Nut or Neith seems to have given us the words night (neet) and beneath; Morgan claims her Druidic Mysteries were long remembered in the Vale of Neath, and Gwyn is remembered there too.

Druidic Mysteries were calendrical, but the calendar also symbolised the human seasons of birth, growth, death and rebirth. Gwyn's livery of red and blue may well have stood for day and night, summer and winter. In an early myth he abducts Creudillad (the earth-maiden) from her outraged husband Gwythyr. Arthur, asked to impose order, decrees that the summer and winter rivals for her hand should battle it out annually. But Arthur himself becomes the winter king in later Arthurian legend, for Melwas or Meleagant steals Guinevere from him and imprisons her in his castle on the Tor, until Lancelot whirls in single-handed to rescue and restore her to her lord, "in due season".

The seasonal element is clear in Tristram's abduction of the willing Isolde; the lovers are able to hide from Mark, her wintry husband, while the leaves of the forest are thick and green; but when the trees are bare, their lair is easily discovered and Tristran must return her, all unwilling, to her lord. Tristram's part is that of the young summer sun; his youth is always emphasised, and many characteristics show him as Gemini. Lancelot is Leo, sun of full summer, peerless, ardent, splendid. He in his turn, abducts Guinevere to his castle Joyous Garde until the seasons turn and she must be given back to Arthur.

Pointless and primitive as all these rapes and counter-rapes may seem on the surface, they hide deeper doctrines. Druid teachings on the purpose of human life were cosmic; the sky interacted with the earth to give a revolving stage of infinite variety, providing not only parable but an actual scenario of experience by which aspiring souls, following their sun-god, could be alchemised into gold. Taliesin's tale tells us as much; he tastes but three drops of a brew made to the recipe of the Druid Pheryllt Order of alchemists, with herbs gathered from every season of the year – and is rendered omniscient, inspired. But that is only the beginning. Only then does he realise that to become god-like will involve him in repeated deaths and rebirths like the sun until he is able, sunlike, to give life and light to others. This in the end he does, rescuing Prince Elphin from prison and by his inspired poetry making his court a renowned centre of bardism.

Alas, the gods of the old religion become the devils of the new, and to Collen, Gwyn was just a demon.

That night Collen prayed that he might be given a place to dwell in for the rest of his life, and an angel told him that he was to descend the Tor "until he saw a road leading on towards the east" when he would that same day meet a horse. This he must mount, and as much land as he could ride round in a day would be his Sanctuary till Doomsday. He found the horse at a place called Rhysfa Maes Cadfarch (the course of the Charger's Field), which we can hardly doubt was Sagittarius on the Pennard Hills, east of the Tor; his chosen Sanctuary must be the Zodiac, thirty miles round, or a day's ride on horseback.

Did not William of Malmesbury describe Glastonbury as "a Heavenly Sanctuary on Earth"? – and though he was ostensibly referring to the Old

Church, one suspects that William was speaking in code. He says for instance "In the pavement may be seen on every side stones designedly interlaid in triangles and squares, under which if I believe some sacred mystery to be contained, I do no injustice to religion.....". The Zodiac reflected on the ground is indeed "A Heavenly Sanctuary on Earth"; its squares are the quadruplicities into which its signs are divided (4 Cardinal, 4 Fixed, 4 Mutable), its triangles the Triplicities (3 Fire, 3 Earth, 3 Air and 3 Water signs). In William's time cathedrals were being adorned with Zodiacs, an indication that they were thought "to do no injustice to religion". Further remarks of his are equally enigmatic. "No-one ever brought hawk or horse within the neighbouring cemetery who did not depart injured, either in them or in himself -". One is reminded of Glastonbury's self-immolating eagle or phoenix, and of Sagittarius' stumbling horse nearby, with its falling rider. As if to confirm these suspicions, he next mentions ordeals of fire and water, and remarks that no building (which could stand for earth) was allowed to keep the light (air?) from the sacred fane. He calls the "church" the Secret of the Lord.

In the life of St Dunstan, written about 1000 AD by a Saxon monk, is another Zodiac clue. "In the royal island of Glastonia the first neophites of Catholic Law, guided by God, found an ancient church constructed (it is said) by no human art, yet prepared by the *very heavens* for the salvation of men".

"Church" and "Kirk" it is worth noting, derive from the same root as "circle". The "Old Church of Glastonbury" seems always to have been there, and built moreover by no human art .... Joseph of Arimathea was eventually credited with its construction, but as we have seen, the legends surrounding his arrival in Glastonbury themselves indicate that the Zodiac's existence was already known, either to him or to his legend-maker.

St Collen is patron of Llangollen (as its name tells us), and the legend of his encounter with the Giantess Virgo has been transported to the famous Horseshoe Pass, no doubt by Celts fleeing into the mountains of Wales to escape the ravages of Saxon and Dane. This giantess killed and ate anyone who attempted the Horseshoe Pass, until Collen determined to rid the place of her. (The Earth Mother Goddess gives life to all, but devours their bodies at death. Was Collen eliminating the older Trinity's only female figure in favour of the all-male Christian Trinity?). Collen boldly met her and asked her what she was doing there. Her answer was intriguing. "It is I, killing myself", she said. They fought and Collen cut off her right arm with his sword, but she picked it up and began to flail him with it until he cut off her remaining arm. At this she cried out to Arthur the Giant to help her from his cave in the Eglwyseg (church) Rocks, but before he could come to her aid, Collen slew her, bathing her blood off himself in a spring known ever since that day as Ffynnon Gollen. And though all this is supposed to have taken place in Wales, it is reassuring to find that Arthur was remembered as her associate, perhaps her consort – as in the Glastonbury Zodiac.

His third encounter with its ancient Trinity is given in the following way. To end the incessant wars between Christians and pagans, a formidable Giant named Bras challenged the pope to find a Christian able to fight him single-handed, stipulating that the vanquished should adopt the victor's faith. The pope, finding no-one who dared to take on this Goliath, was at last divinely directed to Porth Hantwn (Southampton), where he found St Collen who bravely accepted the challenge. At the first encounter, Bras (whose strange name reminds one of Gemini's upraised arm), wounded Collen's *arm*; but with chivalrous generosity Bras broke off the fight, handing him a pot of healing ointment which cured him miraculously at once. Collen, however, determined that his opponent was not to avail himself of his salve, threw the pot into the river, thus gaining an unfair advantage. (One notes that Collen's manners are not up to those of his pagan adversaries). Greatly strengthened he then felled the giant to the ground - which is just where we should expect to find an earth-giant. Bras implored him to save his life, promising him that not only he, but "the whole Greek nation" would consent to become Christian. The pope then baptised him on the spot, and all the Greeks too. This is said to have happened in the wars of Julian the Apostate, but as he belonged to the fourth century and Collen to the seventh, this is a little anachronistic. Baring-Gould supposed Bras to have been a Saracen, and he guessed better than he knew, for Saracens worshipped the stars. In Arthurian legend Solomon's magical ship sailed without oars to the holy city of Sarras, bearing Galahad and Perceval to see the Grail. They did not need to move from the spot, for Sarra means stars; they were in the Cancerian Ship of the Star-city of Avalon, the star-Temple; Bras "the Saracen" is sitting in Solomon's Ship of ancient wisdom as Gemini the Christlike knight, a model of chivalry, suffering yet healing others – hardly needing to be baptised.

It is noteworthy that St Collen finds a use for Sagittarius and baptises Gemini; Virgo is the only one he eliminates. It is difficult to be sure at this distance of time what his attitude to the Zodiac really was. It seems at least from his legends that he knew of it and took it seriously. He even chose it for his Sanctuary. Why "till Domesday?" Presumably because it was expected to last until that final Trumpet-call. We only know these legends through monastic copies of the sixteenth century (the Hafod MS,1536, and

Llanstephan MSS, of 1544), which gives plenty of time for Roman male-orientated Christian copyists to banish Virgo from the Trinity.

I have altered the order of Collen's adventures in order to give the Zodiac Trinity its usual sequence; the last tale is the first in the mediaeval Life. It was after Collen's victory over Bras that he came to Glastonbury, became a monk and eventually was made Abbot. After five years he cursed the local people for their wrong-doing (he is not the only choleric saint in the Celtic calendar by any means) and left the abbey for his solitary cell on the Tor.

One early incident is worthy of mention before we leave him. He was as usual of royal descent, and his mother Ethne (who was Irish) dreamed at his conception that a dove took her heart and bore it up to heaven; it then returned and replaced the vital organ, now embellished with sweet odours. The dove also plays his part, of course, in the conception of the sun-god in the Zodiac.

St PATRICK (c. 373 - 461), Ireland's patron saint was a Briton, born, according to his Tripartite Life, at Nemptor, Ailcluid (Clydeside). His father Calpurnius was a Christian deacon. Nemet indicates a Druid holy place, so no doubt it was one where former Druids embraced Christianity. Later they lived at Bannaventa burniae, somewhere on the west coast, some say Pembroke, some Burnham in Somerset. From here the boy Patrick was kidnapped by pirates and sold as a slave to an Irish landowner and Druid, Miliuc, in Ulster. Both Brigit and Patrick experienced years of slavery – a powerful stimulus to their Christian missions.

After some six years Patrick escaped by ship to Gaul and returned home, but the desire to convert the land of his captivity made him go back to Gaul to study with St Germanus. The Anglo-Saxon Chronicle tells us that he preached in Britain before going to Ireland; Glastonbury claims him indeed as its first Abbot, asserting that he is buried there, a claim now hotly denied by the Irish, who list two Patricks, one for Ireland, one for Glastonbury. One wonders whether Cornish St Petrock is the Glastonbury "Patrick?"

The Abbey even had "St Patrick's Charter", though this is said to be forged. Whatever the truth of all this, Glastonbury was much resorted to by Irishmen as a result of the tradition. If Patrick's home was indeed Burnham, he must have visited the Abbey's Old Church which is only about fourteen miles up the river Brue, and was then the prime centre of British Christianity, and as a Christian with Druid connections he is likely to have known of the Zodiac. Mrs Maltwood adduces one of his legends to show that he did. It occurs in his Tripartite Life as an event that took place in Ireland, not Glastonbury, so I will quote from Whitley Stokes' translation (Vol. 1, p. 91) and let readers judge for themselves.

"Patrick went over the water to Mag Slecht, a place in which was the chief idol of Ireland, namely Cenn (or Cromm) Cruaich, covered with gold and silver, and twelve other idols covered with brass about him. When Patrick saw the idol from the water named Guth-ard (i.e. he lifted up his voice) and when he drew nigh to the idol he raised up his hand to put Jesu's staff upon it, but reached it not, but .... its right side, for to the south was its face, namely to Tara; and the mark of the staff still remains on its left side, and yet the staff did not move out of Patrick's hand. And the earth swallowed up the twelve other images as far as their heads, and they still stand thus in token of the miracle. And he cursed the demon and expelled him into hell."

The exertion made Patrick lose his brooch, but he stripped the heather until he found it, and now "no heather grows in that place."

Patrick founded a church there and left one Mabran, a relative of his, to serve as its priest. This name is suspiciously like the Mabon Son of Modron the Mother, who we shall see later is to be identified with Gemini of the Glastonbury Zodiac; and Mrs Maltwood ascribes the gold and silver on the idol to the sun and moon, Gemini being a sun-god in the Cancerian moon-boat of Argo Navis. His face would be facing south if his head were not bowed, so that it faces west. The name Cromm Cruach means the Bowed One of the Mound - an apt description of Gemini on his hills. In Christian Ireland the Cromm Cruach became notorious as a symbol of cruel paganism; old poems tell how he demanded the blood of sacrificed children in return for good harvests – an ironic reversal of roles if he is in fact a memory of Gemini the suffering self-sacrificing sun-god, and a child himself.

The Tripartite Life of St Patrick, says Whitley Stokes, must have been written about 1000 AD, more than five centuries after Patrick died; plenty of time for a British legend to have become rooted in Irish soil, and for the gods of the old faith to become the devils of the new. The Life contains many instances of Patrick out-doing the Druids at their own magic; one portrays him as burning one recalcitrant Druid to death in a hut by what we would now regard as necromantic means, to show his superiority in magic; other shew him cursing land-owners who would not give him land for his church so effectively that in no time they were reduced to dire poverty. But these legends surely tell us more about the mentality of later monkish scribes than about Patrick's conversion methods; he did not become so beloved by his flock by using fear and hell-fire. Columba said

"Christ is my Druid", showing Christianity as building on and fulfilling the older teachings; this seems much more in keeping with Celtic Christianity's ethos - not reducing others to poverty but embracing it themselves, preferring ascetic hermits' huts to fat abbacies, tilling the soil spade in hand, winning love and respect by healing, feeding and giving shelter to the dispossessed, confronting oppressors unarmed and single-handed and securing justice where they could, invariably protecting hunted animals, starting springs in arid places (perhaps by dowsing?), building sea-walls against tidal erosion, irrigating; encouraging learning, art and crafts with such zeal that it produced a Celtic Renaissance.

Such was Celtic Christianity, lowly, humble, ecological, hard-working. Power-trip Christianity came later, to stain the pages of these saintly lives when, centuries after, they were written down.

Dogmatic, pompous missions, such as Augustine's in Kent and Wilfred's in York, flickered out and failed, and had to be rekindled from Iona by gentler Celtic hands. As to Patrick it seems the Druidic methods he used were by nature-parable, not by fire and brimstone, if his legend of using the shamrock leaf to demonstrate the Trinity's Three-in-One is anything to go by. Not only the method but the concept of the Trinity was druidic, and not new to his hearers. Nor were "St Patrick's Purgatories" – for fogous or underground caves were already in use by Druids to demonstrate the passage of the soul through death to new life; it was well known to the ancient world that they taught the immortality of the soul.

Another suspiciously Zodiacal tale about St Patrick tells how he dug up the bones of a great giant, brought him to life and made him work for him digging the foundation of his monasteries. This tale is told of other Celtic saints also. Were they building Christianity on the bones of the Glastonbury Giants?

St BEON, said to be an Irish Monk, was called by an angel to go and meet St Patrick. But the latter told him to become a hermit and keep on walking until his staff budded into a tree. This duly happened at Meare, some three miles north-west of Glastonbury. So here he settled, finding it suitable in every way, except that there was no drinking water, which his acolyte Pincius had to fetch daily from a distance. (This is distinctly odd, for Meare as its name implies was once a large lake; Meare's famous Iron Age Lake Village was built on piles above it, and the villagers presumably found its water sufficiently drinkable. In mediaeval times long after St Beon, it was still there, and became the Abbey's great fishery. Are we being alerted to a Secret?

One hot day Pincius, wearied with water-carrying, fell asleep and had his pitcher stolen – or said he had – and though it was later returned, Beon took the hint and in the manner of Celtic saints caused a spring of pure water to gush forth next his hermitage. Is Pincius Glastonbury's Water-Carrier – Aquarius?

Beon's second tale could also be a Zodiac hint. He built a causeway across the marsh to Glastonbury, and one night on his way to prayer at the Old Church was confronted by a fearsome demon. Unable to pass, he shouted "Bloody Beast! What are you doing here?" "Waiting for you," snarled the monster ominously. But Beon fearlessly raised his staff and thrashed him with it so soundly that the "beast" sank without trace into a bottomless pool. Was this the Piscean Whale, its tail drawn by the river Brue near Beon's causeway? Or Capricorn, whose forefoot sinks into the Hartlake nearby? For Capricorn's goat has often been seen as the Devil, horned and goat-footed, and a goat has long been said to haunt the Tor.

Beon has a church that was once dedicated to him at Glastonbury; but the Roman church often substituted later Catholic saints for Celtic dedications, and St Benedict has taken over from the hermit. This church is on the sunset line from Stonehenge that sweeps west down the abbey nave over Arthur's grave; its tower can be seen between the turrets of the abbey's Lady Chapel, looking west.

Beon may well have been sent by Patrick to convert an old Druid grove at Meare to Christianity, for apparently Beon's oak there was famous. So his budding staff, like Joseph's, signified the planting of the new Faith on the remains of the old. Two corbels in his church show him as a bishop holding this sprouting staff, in defiance of the usurping St Benedict.

ST BRIGIT OF KILDARE is tenaciously claimed by Glastonbury as having come here to visit St Patrick - though by all accounts she was only born some seven years before his death. However, William of Malmesbury wrote that "Brigit, who came to Glastonbury in the year 488, returned home again after some little stay in an island called Beckery, having left behind her certain important relics, namely her hood, beads, handbell and weaving tools, which are preserved there in her memory." But he wrote six hundred years after her death, when these "relics" had for long been used to impress the many Irish monks who came to Glastonbury. Fourteeth century John of Glastonbury recorded that William's authority for this statement was Gildas, way back in the seventh century, but if Gildas did write on Brigit, the book has long disappeared; nor do his extant works mention her.

Whether she actually came or not, Chalice Well claimed to have her

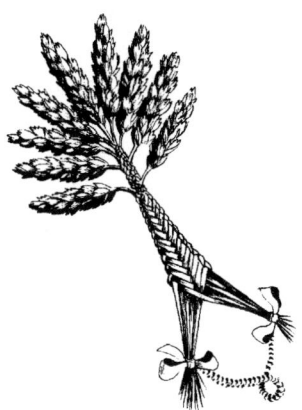

ancient cow-bell until the 1920's, when, sadly, it mysteriously disappeared. Due to the large Irish contingent at the Abbey, she became popular enough to be carved with her cow on its west door, and again on the Tor's tower. They must have built the small Celtic shrine at Beckery (a name meaning Little Ireland), and when it collapsed, Dunstan built a larger chapel over it and dedicated it to St Brigit. Fields and a well at Beckery are still called after her.

Brigit's beginnings could hardly have been humbler. Her father, a landowner called Dubtach, begot her on one of his slave-girls, Brotessa; but his jealous wife insisted that this obvious rival should begone before the child was born. Dubtach reluctantly sold Brotessa to a Druid friend of kindly disposition who owned a prosperous farm some thirty miles north near Dundalk, where he knew the babe would be well cared for. With Druidic insight, Brotessa's new master prophesied: "Marvellous will be the child that is in her womb; the bondmaid will bring forth a daughter conspicuous and radiant, who will shine like a sun among the stars of heaven; her like will not be known on earth. Blest be the child born neither in the house nor out of it." And sure enough, Brigit was born at sunrise when her mother stepped over the threshold with a milk-pail in her hand. They washed the baby in it; one might say she was delivered with the milk.

Her reputation for learning must have begun with her Druid master's teaching, which imbued her with a great love of Nature and an understanding of its divine symbolism. But her mother was a Christian, converted perhaps like so many slaves by St Patrick, who preached the equality of all men in the sight of God. So she was exposed at once in early youth to the old faith and the new, and seems to have successfully harmonised them both. For did she not join the ancient Druid centre at Kildare, and help the vestal virgins keep the perpetual fires alight? Kildare means cell of the oak, and a hoary oak tree there was much venerated by the people. Nor was it long before she began to graft Christianity on to its ancient trunk, persuading the vestals to keep the traditional fire burning in honour of the pentecostal flame of the Holy Spirit. It blazed on for centuries, despite the disapproval of a Norman bishop, who extinguished it momentarily as a pagan survival; for as soon as his back was turned the Brigittine nuns relit it, to popular rejoicing.

Sacked many times by the Danes after Brigit's death, Kildare still survived as one of the chief churches of Ireland, though its precious library that could have told us so much was burned.

Twelfth century Gerald of Wales visited it, describing it thus: "Since Brigit's glorious departure, nineteen nuns have formed the society. Each nun has care of the fire for a single night ... It is surrounded by a hedge of stakes and brushwood, forming a circle which no man may enter ... Moreover, it is only lawful for women to blow the fire, and they must use bellows, not their own breath."

One is reminded of the Cauldron of Ceridwen, whose fire was gently warmed by the breath of nine maidens, in Taliesin's poem "the Spoils of Annwn," and of the Druidesses of the Isle of Sena near Brest mentioned by Pomponius Mela as "the abode of priestesses holy in perpetual virginity, nine in number, who by their charms are able to raise the winds and seas, to turn themselves into what animals they will, to cure wounds and diseases incurable by others, and to know and predict the future."

Brigit too was credited with command over the weather, and with healing the sick, even lepers. If corn-dollies – known as Bride- or Brigit-babies– were put to bed with a poker, this ensured good crops, such were her powers of fertility; women prayed to her in childbirth for safe delivery. She could curse too in true Druidic fashion. She begged a bishop for corn when her barns were empty, and was told he had none to give. But she had spied out his store, and her scornful disbelief so withered him that he gave her twelve wagon-loads to see the back of her.

Once she went to beg a local chief for land for a new nunnery, promising in return to pray for his soul. "Pray rather that I live long on this earth, and vanquish all my enemies," he said. " It shall be done", said she without a qualm, for it was customary for Druids to protect their chiefs with their magic.

Tales like these have persuaded some mythologists that Brigit never lived, but was in fact the great Celtic goddess Brigantia in Christian guise. And clearly much of the veneration for the fertility goddess did devolve on Brigit in this time of transition; but her legends breathe such a warm, witty, compassionate, strong-minded, capable human being with a touch of the virago about her, that it is easier to see a real person beneath the goddess she became.

Brigit, even while she was a slave, was an incorrigible giver; that she had nothing of her own to give deterred her not a whit; she happily gave away her master's goods. Perhaps this is why he returned her to her father after a time? Delighted as Dubtach was to have his daughter back, his wife soon transferred her jealousy of Brotessa to Brigit, and the house became a battle-ground. Not only was Brigit given all the hardest, dirtiest tasks, but the lengthening queues of beggars at the door became a bone of contention. The angels were hard put to it to answer Brigit's prayers for miraculous return of missing sides of bacon, eggs and loaves of bread in time, and when they occasionally failed, Brigit (never an abject slave) stood her ground, saying she was only "giving back to Christ what was his own."

At last her step-mother insisted that either she or Brigit must go; so the sorrowing father took her to his cousin Dunlang, King of Leinster, who had been baptised by St Patrick. Leaving Brigit in his chariot in charge of his jewelled sword, he went to describe her incomparable virtues to the king, but was horrified when he came to fetch her to find his sword gone. She had been unable to resist the pleading of a beggar at the king's gate, and said "Christ has taken it." Dunlang, however, mollified him, saying "she has more merit than either of us," and laughing, engaged her in sprightly conversation, charmed by her beauty, her ready wit and self-possession. But when asked if he would take this remarkable "slave", he refused, saying: "so free-handed a slave is too expensive a luxury for any but a saint".

In despair, Dubtach set her free, and invited suitors to marry her. But she refused them all, even putting out one eye, so it is said, to mar her beauty. Another version of this is more likely – that her brother, furious at the slave's rejection of suitors so above her station, gave her a black eye.

A determined virgin, she went to a Christian household, where she soon mastered Latin, and then gathering seven more virgins (escaped slaves?) about her went to Kildare.

Her outstanding character ensured that in time she became abbess of her nunnery. It prospered and grew, and so did her herds of cows, for each free woman who joined had to bring one with her. Her herd's yield increased miraculously, for Brigit sang to them as she milked, so that when beggars importuned, she could milk the contented creatures three times a day.

Men joined her community as well, after the pattern of the emerging

Celtic Church, building and working in the fields while the nuns baked, milked, wove their garments and even brewed ale for them. Kildare became a busy oasis of peace and plenty in the midst of endemic tribal wars and the starvation they brought. Learning and exquisite metalwork flourished within its boundaries, and Brigit brought new life to the whole district, for we are told that when a farmer fell ill, she sent her monks and nuns to nurse him and run his farm until he recovered.

Brigit loved to give feasts to the needy; the tale goes that when a riotous party of beggars had drunk her ale dry and still demanded more, she told them there was only her bathwater left and if they were still thirsty they could drink that.

She was certainly a matriarch, and sometimes overdid it. Her Irish temper flared when a woman who had brought apples for the nuns objected at seeing them distributed to beggars; Brigit cursed her orchard so that it withered and died. And there was the sad occasion when she gave away her faithful monk Conlaith's vestments, embroidered for him by her nuns. He deserved better of her, for his beautiful Celtic metalwork had long enriched the community. Outraged, he determined to leave and go on pilgrimage to Rome. She, shocked at losing him, threatened him with a dreadful fate if he left, But he went nonetheless, and was devoured by wolves on the way.

But despite these lapses from grace, her rule was generally generous and just; it may be that these incidents are part of the mantle of the ancient goddess in her vengeful aspect, that fell upon Brigit, her namesake. Will it redress the balance to record a humbler legend of the great abbess? When some of her nuns demurred at having to wash the feet and pare the toe-nails of the elderly sisters, she rolled up her sleeves and performed the task herself, reminding them how Christ had washed the feet of his disciples, and that she, at least, was his slave.

Her reputation grew until kings and bishops came to ask her advice. She travelled many rough Irish miles– being thrown from her chariot more than once – to reprove chieftains for misbehaviour, and to obtain land from them for new communities. Before she died it was said that she had 13,000 novitiates under her charge.

Though there is no hint that Brigit ever left Ireland, save for the legends of Glastonbury's Irish monks, one can well imagine why she became so popular here. In her day the great pagan goddesses were being submerged under the rising tide of Christianity, providing no powerful earth-mother to take their place – for the Virgin Mary was too meek to compete with the old Virago. Brigit, who soon after her death was deified as the Mother of

God, and the Mary of the Gaels, was just the robust sort of goddess, with no hint of Eastern feminine subservience to men, to fill the gap.

For was not all Avalon owned by Virgo, the Zodiac's Great Mother? Her effigy, four miles long, is outlined from bonnet to hem by the river Cary, so she is the old Mother Carey or Ceridwen, the British Ceres, queen of the land, its cows and its corn. On her breast a huge prehistoric mound called Wimble Toot forms her nipple, and was doubtless a centre for pagan harvest thanksgivings, for Toot or twt, old Welsh for a look-out mound, is the same word as teat. Babcary on her swelling womb still has a legend that a Royal Child was hidden here - for our Virgin is also the mother of all living. Annis Hill near her head, and Ansford on her feet make her also Black Annis, the old British witch - and British Anna, Britannia. There is even a Britannia inn at Castle Cary, by the river's source, the Seven Lady Springs.

Brigit, who could command the weather, before whom even chieftains quailed, must have seemed a worthy successor to the old Virgin-goddess; had they not been told that her name "Bride" meant Bride of Christ? The ancient customs could now be addressed confidently to her; the wells decorated, beacon-fires lit, corn-dollies dedicated, and prayers for fertility, safe delivery in childbirth, or from tyrants, could now be directed instead to all-powerful Brigit. From Brigantia to Brigit was hardly a change of name.

Brigantia
3rd Cent
Romano-
British.
Birren
Dumfrieshire

CHAPTER 3

ST DAVID OF WALES was born sometime about 500 AD and lived to a great age, nearly spanning the century. He, like St Patrick, is said to have visited Glastonbury, and much sun-myth has collected about him. His mother was St Nunn; his father the Welsh King Sandde, or Seint, was obviously too saintly to have anything to do with David's conception, thus hinting at a Virgin Birth. His family traced back to Avallach and the Holy family in any case, and one of David's legends tells how he built an addition to Glastonbury's Old Church and was about to dedicate it when Jesus appeared to him in a vision and told him that there was no need, as He Himself had long ago dedicated it to the Blessed Virgin His Mother. (Rumours have long circulated there that "no other hands but those of the Lord Himself" built the Old Church, and that the Virgin was indeed buried here).

Those who find this a bit steep (like the Tor, and the legend of her Assumption from its summit) may prefer to see this as a clue to the Zodiac, the Oldest Church in Britain, made by Nature or the Creator Himself, and dedicated to Virgo, Mother Earth, to whom all land on this planet belongs.

The name of Biblical Joshua, son of Nun, is translated as "son of a fish"; so David son of St Nunn, is equally aquatic – in fact he was entitled "Vir Aquaticus", – being born during a great sea-storm, so it is said. We are told that St Nunn gave birth to him under a rock that was split by lightning, whirled into the air and landed at her unharmed feet; the marks of her hands they say can still be seen on it as she clung to it in her birth-pangs. A truly cosmic event, St David's birth!

So in our Zodiac Trinity, the Libran Dove hurtles earthward from Sagittarius' godhead towards Virgo. Hurtle Pool was once on its wing, though it is now, like many old ponds, filled in. But the very name David means Dove.

"Duw Dovydd gives me a ray of inspiration from the Cauldron of Ceridwen" sang 6th century Taliesin the Bard. Duw Dovydd was the Druidic God the Creator, the sun – or the sun behind the sun – seeding the earth with life by the Logos or sun-ray, the Word. God dived, or to use the obsolete past participle, He *dove*.

The sea-storm is Ceridwen's boiling cauldron from which all life emerges; the lightning is the Logos descending to enlighten men by the birth of an enlightened Man. There seems little doubt that David's birth-legend derives from Druidic Zodiac teachings. Can it be accident that the

Dove's head in our Zodiac is at Barton St David? Or that there is a mediaeval statue to St David of Wales in its churchyard? Over the chancel arch is an old picture of another David, the Jewish King, relaying a divine octave from heaven to earth on his seven-stringed harp. Were the parishioners confused? Not a bit of it. All Davids are Messengers of the Most High – Logos-Doves.

St David, Vir Aquaticus. Is it accident or Zodiac design that this "son of a Fish" should be remembered as helping to build the Abbey which lies between Pisces, ruled by Neptune, and Aquarius, ruled by Uranus of the Lightning-strike?

By strange coincidence, I watched on St David's day a David Attenborough nature film of diving sea-birds in slow motion, which also featured whirl-winds and waterspouts. Except for the name of the film-maker, it had nothing to do with St David; but as I was writing this chapter at the time it was difficult not to see the Dove hurtling from heaven and David's birth-storm in these shots, or to feel that the saint was sending an encouraging message. I also received a bunch of daffodils – David's flower– that day. For David the Dove is above all the communicator; the generic name for doves is Columbidae - column or communication-cord. Early telephones were daffodil-shaped, and whirlwinds and water-spouts are continuous columns stretching from heaven to earth.

The curious legend of St David's altar has Zodical overtones. With St Padarn he is said to have made a pilgrimage to Jerusalem, where its patriarch made him Archbishop of Wales (a Welsh dig at the papacy, which claimed monopoly in such appointments). He was also given "a consecrated altar in which the body of our Lord once lay". As this was presumably Joseph of Arimathea's rock-cut tomb, it was difficult to see how it could be transported back to Britain; indeed, David said as much. No problem! On David's return, it flew through the air with the greatest of ease and landed at his feet. It took the form of a sapphire, in two semi-circles.

A "stone", blue as the sky, in two hemispheres, falling to earth at Glastonbury - what can this be but the Zodiac? It also uttered oracles; the Zodiac is a system of prophecy. And when David died we are told that it was covered in skins and hidden, so that it was never seen again – "nor could any man tell of its colour or the substance of which it was made".

The Twelve Hides of Glastonbury, twelve animal-hides or Hidden Figures! It did indeed contain "the body of our Lord", in Gemini's Christlike effigy on Dundon and Lollover hills. (This tale comes from Rhigyfarch's Life of St David, 1095 AD, retold in Waite's "The Holy Grail".)

The old tradition that Glastonbury is the New Jerusalem perhaps stems from David's "altar". The "New Jerusalem" of the Book of Revelations is also Zodiacal, with its twelve gates and twelve jewelled foundation-walls, whose precious stones all correspond to the signs of the Zodiac.

Why was this "altar", and even its memory lost? David died just before Augustine brought Roman Christianity to England in 601, when the slow but inexorable process of suppressing the Celtic church began. In saying that St David was crowned Archbishop by the Patriarch of the Eastern Church the Welsh were defiantly claiming an older form of the Faith independent of Rome. But he hardly needed to learn of the Glastonbury Zodiac from such a source; he was surely too well versed in his native traditions for that. He is said for instance to have found the site for St David's cathedral in Pembroke by the flight of his pet dove which always perched on his shoulder, and which on this occasion flew ahead of him until it finally rested in a bush. So many churches have bird and animal guides to their foundation-sites that this must have been ancient geomancy at work – a custom faithfully followed by early Christians. Druids like other primordial peoples regarded the movement of birds and animals as divine omens, a "right-brain" attitude from which we have now long since ceased to benefit.

At another time at a vast concourse of monks in the open air the speakers could neither be seen nor heard by those on the outside of the crowd, elevated as they were only on a pile of clothing which muffled their speech. David, following Druidic practice, moved them to a nearby ancient mound where all could be clearly heard and seen, and a successful Gorsedd was had by all.

ST PADARN, c. 480 - 550, David's companion in pilgrimage, also received a gift from the Patriarch of Jerusalem - a richly bejewelled cope. On his return "the tyrant Arthur:" demanded it. Padarn stoutly refused, and by magical means buried our beloved King in the ground "up to his neck" until he promised to leave the saint's cell in peace.

What can this irreverent tale be but a memory of Arthur-Sagittarius, buried in the ground at Baltonsborough?

Arthur is often portrayed unsympathetically in these Celtic saints' Lives; this is a puzzle, for most of the Lives were written by Welsh monks, and for the Welsh as for the Cornish and Bretons, Arthur was a supreme folk-hero. One can only speculate that by the 1100's when these Lives were being written - some 500 years or more after they were lived - the Norman Catholic grip had such a hold on the scriptorium, that it was safer to trim one's sails when mentioning him. For Arthur, it was rumoured, was not dead but would one day return to free his Celts from foreign domination in both church and state. At that time Arthurian and Grail legends were also being written and becoming enormously popular in the freer air of secular courts of France and Britain; but though the tales were ostensibly pious (knights invariably said mass at daybreak and showed great respect to the hermits who appear at every turn to advise and admonish them) it was a piety that made the Roman Church suspicious of subcutaneous heresy. The Grail Mass, as we have seen, contained Secret Words not in the Roman Rite; those barefoot hermits breathed the lowly spirit of Celtic Christianity; the legends were circulated by emigrant bards and troubadours, tainted in southern France by the heinous heresy of Catharism.

Welsh historian-monks were in a quandary, for by the 1100's they were under Norman priors and abbots; no Welshman was allowed such an office, nor indeed any cure of souls in those harsh times. Yet like all oppressed peoples they needed to remember their greater past, so under the beady eye of their abbots, they put together what scraps of saintly folk-lore that still survived, much of it apocryphal, some of it in code, to recreate a past that was undoubtedly spiritually great.

An old piece of Zodiacal Lore has attached itself to St David at Llandewi Brevi, the scene of his great church conference. It was said that he possessed two horned oxen who had dragged a monstrous beast out of a lake. David struck dead the villain who had let this pest loose after it had been captured with great difficulty. An inscription to this effect was found by Edward Lluwyd over the chancel of Llandewi Brevi church, and the sexton showed him a huge ox-horn, so heavy it must have been a fossil, to prove it. Dinely in 1684 comments that this ox 'had so large a head that the pith of one of its horns would equal in bigness a man's thigh". It must have been a fossil aurochs, Bos Primigenius.

David also had a bell called Bangu, made by St Gildas, who was apparently a notable bell-founder. Another legend goes that David's two oxen were put to hauling stones for his church at Llandewi Brevi, but one fell dead with the effort of pulling them up a steep mountain, whereupon the other, bewailing its lost companion, bellowed nine times so loudly that it blasted a level track through the mountain and was thus able to haul the stones by itself.

These tales, however, belong to pre-Christian times. The Triad entitled the Three Chief Master Works of the Island of Britain goes thus;

The Ship of Nevydd Nav Neivion, which carried in it a male and female of all living, when the lake of waters burst forth;

The drawing of the avanc to land out of the lake by the branching oxen of Hu Gadarn, so that the lake burst no more;

And the stones of Gwyddon Ganhebon, on which were read the arts and sciences of the world.

David's oxen are really Hu Gadarn's, the sun-god of the Cymry, who led them from the east to Britain in the dawn of time, teaching them the arts of agriculture and, it would seem, irrigation. He also taught the Triad method of remembering their history. (Gwyddon Ganhebon is represented as the first poet, who first inscribed letters on stone. The cuneiform Broad Arrow? Or Ogham?).

It is tempting to see these three Master Works as memorials of the Glastonbury Zodiac - especially as we already suspect David to have known of it as the "stone from heaven". The Ship Argo, or Ark, figures there, and the Avanc could well be the Piscean Whale or Leviathon, drawn out of what was previously a lake by Hu's Taurean oxen - a notable feat of irrigation. The Awen's Broad Arrow is also implied by the masts of the Ship, illuminating the Gemini Babe. And David's bell, Bangu, was originally the name of one of Hu's oxen!

Medieval marble, St Mary, Chessington, Surrey

St NUNN or NONNITA, St David's mother, deserves a paragraph to herself. Baring Gould's version is somewhat different to that already given. She was the daughter of one Cunr, whose castle, Caer Gawch, was a British camp on St David's headland. In this account she was raped by Sandde, a petty chief (how has saintly King Seint fallen!). The details of the birth-storm are the same, but the split rock becomes a menhir near Porth Cleis which was afterwards made the cornerstone of a chapel which is still there but now ruinous. The babe David was baptised by Bishop Beluc (note the Bel in the name), in the well of Porth Cleis. So it would seem that David founded his cathedral at his birthplace.

St Nun is also remembered at Altarnun, Cornwall and at Bradstone nearby, where they say she was martyred by Druids on the "broad stone".

Her association with such antiquities as a British Camp, menhirs and Druidic rites heighten the suspicion that the mantle of the pre-Christian Earth-mother has fallen upon her; Virgin soil ever reaped or raped, yet ever undefiled. The hint of the creative forces of a pre-Christian Trinity at work in the birth-storm is strengthened by three names carved on a stone in St Cuby's church, Tregony – Nonnita, Ercilius, Virigatus. Nonnita, Hercules the semi-divine hero and The Virile Begetter or Creator?

ST CARANTOC, whose day is celebrated on May 16th, is another 6th century saint born of the line of South Welsh or Silurian kings who traced their ancestry like St David to the Holy Family. In the words of his 12th century Life now in the British Museum - "Blessed Carantoc, son of Cereticus ... was high-placed according to the dignity of this world, so easy is it to trace his descent from Mary, the mother of our Lord ....".

Descending from kings, he must have inherited the Royal Secret of the Zodiac, so it is fascinating to find that he like St David received a mysterious "altar" from heaven. Let the scribe tell this miracle in his own words.

"And Christ gave him from on high an honourable altar, the colour of which no man understood; and afterwards he came to the river Severn to sail across it, and cast his altar into the sea, and it went before him where God willed it to come. At that time Cato and Arthur were reigning in that country, dwelling in Dindrarthou" (Arthur's dun or fortress, thought to be Dunster) "and Arthur came wandering round to find a serpent, most fierce, huge and terrible, which had laid waste twelve parts of the land of Carrum" (Carhampton near Minehead?) and Carantoc came and saluted Arthur, who rejoiced and received a blessing from him.

Carantoc asked Arthur whether he had heard where his altar had come to shore, and Arthur replied "If I am paid for it, I will tell thee"; and he said, "What dost thou ask to be done?" He answered, "That thou shouldst take away the serpent that is close to thee, if thou art a servant of God, that we may see.". Then blessed Carantoc prayed to the Lord; and straightaway the serpent came with a great noise, like a calf running to its mother. And it bent its head before the servant of God like a servant obeying its master, with humble heart and downcast eyes. And he put his stole around its neck, and led it like a lamb, neither did it lift its wings or claws; and its neck was like the neck of a seven-year-old bull, so that the stole could scarcely go round it. Then they led it together to the citadel, and saluted Cato, and were well received by him. And he led that serpent to the middle of the hall, to feed it before the people, and they tried to kill it. But the saint did not suffer it to be killed, because he said that it came by the word of God to destroy the sinners that were in Carrum, and that he might shew the power of God through it. And afterwards it went outside the gate of the citadel, and Carantoc loosened it and commanded it to hurt none, and it went out and injured none, as the appointment of God said. And Carantoc took up the altar which Arthur had thought of making into a table, but whatever was placed upon it was immediately thrown to a distance. And the king asked him to receive Carrum as a perpetual possession by a written deed, and afterwards he built a church there.

Afterwards there came to him a voice from Heaven, bidding him to cast his altar into the sea; then he sent Cato and Arthur to ask about the altar, and they were told that it had come to land at the mouth of the Guellit (the Willet which gives its name to the village of Williton near Watchet); and the king said, "Give him again twelve pieces of land, where the altar was found". Afterwards came Carantoc and built a church there, and the city (monastery) was called Carrov".

This last paragraph reads like a repetition, but helps define the landing-site further by mentioning the little river Willet. This part of the Somerset coast was much favoured by Welsh missionaries, whether they sailed on stone altars or by more conventional means; it is rich in Welsh saintly dedications. The same paragraph also gives an intriguing hint that what is really being recorded is the Glastonbury Zodiac. The serpent devastated twelve parts of Carrum; the king granted twelve pieces of land to Carantoc for rendering it harmless. This is too like Arviragus' grant of the Twelve Hides of Glastonbury to Joseph of Arimathea to be meaningless accident.

Let us examine the tale for further clues. We are already alerted to Zodiac possibilities through St David's altar that came hurtling down from the sky; Carantoc's was also given him "from on high". Christ was connected with both gifts. And is it not significant that Arthur knew the whereabouts of Carantoc's hidden altar? And that he wanted it for a table? The only one we associate with Arthur is of course the Round Table, or the Zodiac. The interesting detail that it threw everything placed upon it to a distance could be a clue to its great size - also that it was thirty miles away from Carhampton. The phrase "Arthur came wandering round" reads more like the circular wanderings of Sagittarius than the progress of a king. The serpent led into the middle of the hall then becomes Draco, circling in mid-heaven round the Pole-star.

Is "Carrum" then merely the old name of Carhampton, or is it also a convenient name for conveying coded information? I submit that as Car was the Roman Earth-Goddess, Virgin-soil to whom as Virgo the whole Zodiac belonged (Mother Carey, all drawn by the river Cary), the name of Carrum was chosen for its power to convey secrets. Cornish "carrick", Welsh "Carreg" and our English "crag" are the very bones of the Earth-Mother.

Carantoc, unlike churchmen today, wouldn't kill Draco, symbol of Zodiac Wisdom, recognising that "the serpent had been sent by God". Enriched by Druid Lore in astronomy and astrology, a royal inheritor of their "greater Secret, known to few", he saw Christianity not as repudiating the divine wisdom - system of his ancestors, but as re-stating and fulfilling it. With commendable subtlety he said that "it came that he might shew the power of God through it"; a statement that could be taken two ways, thus passing uncensored under the eye of successive Saxon and Norman abbots of the Roman Church.

While in Ireland he is said to have helped St Patrick reform the ancient laws, the Senchus Mor. He is remembered there as Cairnech, who performed many miracles of healing and founded a colony of monks at Dulane, "of Britons of lasting fame". They seem to have been a jolly crew ...". Early these men quaff their metheglin, they are the congregation of Cairnech", says an old couplet.

He healed Tenenan, son of an Irish king; a handsome young man, he had contracted leprosy to escape the pressing attentions of the ladies, for he desired to become a monk. Carantoc made him take a bath and scoured him clean. "It's conceited I shall be with my lovely skin", grumbled Tenenan, not well pleased. He then insisted on bathing Carantoc, who was naturally reluctant. It appeared that he wore seven iron belts about his body, next the skin - and as he took his leprous bath these snapped and fell off. "Never mind", he said, "these bands can easily be rivetted again". "Not if all the blacksmiths were to try would they succeed", retorted Tenenan. After this they praised God, and made fellowship.

What are we to make of this? One iron belt as a monastic hardship is a literal possibility, but seven? Hardly. I suspect that they were the seven planetary orbits - Druidic star-lore that in a Christian view still bound Carantoc; Druids were still powerful in the Ireland of that time. And "blacksmiths" meant the influential Druidic Order of the Pheryllt, the chemists or alchemists of those days, when the secrets of iron-working were of the Mysteries.

Was Tenenan telling Carantoc that their ancient power was on the wane, and Christianity's star on the ascendant?

Further hints of Druidic practices follow Carantoc into his cave of Edilu or Ogof Grannog at Llangranog, where he retired for a time as a hermit. It is a "fogou" believed to be three miles long, emerging as a cave northward at Cym Tydi. Druids used these fogous for rites demonstrating the passage of the sun through death to new life at the winter solstice; Carantoc it seems adapted the former rite to demonstrate the death and resurrection of Christ, "the New Sun" as Gildas calls him. The three miles perhaps represented the three days in the tomb.

Carantoc also has a rock resembling a chair, called Eisteddfa Granog near the creek below his cave, and a holy well, now called Ffynnon Fair and given to Our Lady. His brother St Tyssul is commemorated at Tysilio-gogo, the next parish.

He is represented in stained-glass in St Carantoc's church at Crantock in Cornwall with a dove holding a wood-shaving in its beak, because when he first fled his father's court as a beggar, wondering where to go and what to do, he was whittling a staff when a dove flew down and carried off the shavings. He followed it to see where the angelic bird would drop them, and there he built the "city" (monastery) of Carrov.

CHAPTER 4

THE GRAIL-STONE OF "PARZIVAL"

Where else but in the lives of St Carantoc and David can we find a tradition of an oracular stone fallen from heaven? Why, in Wolfram von Eschenbach's "Parzival", written oddly enough in Bavaria about 1200 AD.

Here the Stone becomes the Grail: Parzival being the only Grail legend to designate the Sacred Vessel thus. Scholars still puzzle endlessly on this strange anomaly, but they do so without benefit of the Glastonbury Zodiac, under whose umbrella all apparently contradictory descriptions of the Grail can shelter without quarrelling.

The passage which describes the Grail-Stone is perhaps its clearest identification with the Glastonbury Zodiac in all Grail legends, and is therefore worth quoting. The ascetic hermit Trevrizent acquaints Parzival with its secret:

"A heathen, Flegetanis, had achieved high renown for his learning. This scholar of Nature was descended from Solomon and born of a family which had long been Israelite until baptism became our shield against the fire of Hell ... The heathen Flegetanis could tell us how all the stars set and rise again and how long each one revolves before it reaches its starting-point once more. To the circling course of the stars man's affairs and destiny are linked. Flegetanis saw with his own eyes in the constellations things he was shy to talk about, hidden mysteries. He said there was a thing called the Grail whose name he had read clearly in the stars.

"A host of angels left it on the earth and then flew away up over the stars. Was it their innocence that drew them away? Since then baptised men have had the task of guarding it, and with such chaste discipline that those who are called to the service of the Grail are always noble men". Thus wrote Flegetanis of these things. Kyot, the wise master, set about to trace this tale in Latin books, to see where there ever had been a people, dedicated to purity and worthy of caring for the Grail. He read the chronicles of the lands, in Britain and elsewhere, in France and in Ireland, and in Anjou he found the tale ...".

Flegetanis must have come across the L iber Melkini. Or a version of the secret Zodiac which fails to mention Joseph of Arimathea; – for Joseph is totally absent from Wolfram's Parzifal.

One cannot blame Wolfram for passing over Britain as the source of these secrets, for in his day it was but part of the Angevin Empire under Henry II and his son Richard Lionheart, and the western coast of France from Aquitaine to Brittany had long been the refuge of British bards and the main repository of their sad Arthurian lays, so that they were known, sung and remembered there better than in their homeland, torn for centuries by invading Angles, Saxons, Danes, and lastly Normans. Wolfram knew nothing of British history or even its geography, certainly nothing of its Druidic prehistory and philosophy - though many of his misspelt place-names are traceable to Britain. Parzival le Waleis the Grail-seeker, is obviously Perceval the Welsh or Briton, for instance, and "Utepandragun" can only be the legendary father of Arthur, Uther Pendragon. Gawan and Lanzilot are recognisable, and Arthur himself presides overall, though his seat Wolfram imagines to be at Nantes. In the place-name Famorgan one can dimly recognise the faery realm of Arthur's half-sister, the enchantress Morgan le Faye - and so on. (Glamorgan in South Wales). There can be no doubt that though the intriguing Saracen element in Wolfram's work gives a welcome astrological emphasis to the Grail, the warp on which he wove was of British origin - whether he learnt of it through the elusive Flegetanis, or from Chretien de Troyes as scholars think. I suspect the prime influence in the sudden resurgence of Arthurian legend's popularity to have been Eleanor, firstly queen of France and then of Britain as wife of Henry II – who must have been entranced by British minstrel lays in girlhood at her father's court of Aquitaine – and thus was perfectly placed to receive both mystery-streams, Eastern and Western Druidic. She seems to have passed her excitement on to her daughters Blanche of Castile and Marie de Champagne, Chretien de Troyes' patron.

Welsh records assert that the very Round Table itself was brought to Britain from Brittany – by one Rhys ap Tudwr – and not until 1087, after the Norman Conquest. It comes as quite a shock to find this essential article of furniture arriving on the Arthurian scene so late; until we recognise it as a secret code-word for the Glastonbury Zodiac. It was the *memory* of this Zodiac that was restored to Britain from Brittany, in the wake of William's fierce Breton contingent who fought with him, thirsting to regain the lands lost to them under the Saxons. From Brittany too come most of our memorials of Britain's Celtic saints, related as many were – at least in legend – to Arthur. Numbers of them escaped to Brittany, either to live as hermits in its virgin forests or to minister to their fellow-emigres there in the 5th - 6th centuries. Their relatedness to Arthur may or may not be factual, but it was certainly symbolic - for Celtic Christianity and Arthurian legend are but two sides of the same coin, an alloy of Druidic star-wisdom fused with a poetic interpretation of Christianity.

Wolfram's hermit gave Parzival fragments of their teachings in the following passage, also from Book 9 (Metric translation).

But the hermit again made answer "Thy doubt I will put away
O'er my falsehood thou canst bemoan thee if the thing be not as I say;
For the EARTH was Adam's mother; of the EARTH was Adam fed,
And I ween, though a man she bore here, yet still was the Earth a maid.
Nor on earth shall aught be purer than a maiden undefiled,
Think how pure must be a maiden, since God was a maiden's child!
Two men have been born of maidens, since God hath the likeness ta'en
Of the son of the first Earth-maiden, since to help us He aye was fain."

Virgo's answer from the Zodiac to the Christian doctrine of the Virgin Birth. Thus Wolfram's hermit marries ancient Star-lore to Christianity; For Christ (the True Sun as 6th cent Gildas called him), is born like the reborn sun of the year, at the winter solstice; and the sun rises at this season from the womb of Virgo's stars in the south-east.

The hermit also vouchsafes more secrets of the Grail-stone to his ardent pupil:

"Many brave knights dwell with the Grail at Munsalvaesche. When they ride out, as they often do, it is to seek adventure. They do so for their sins, these templars ... A valiant host lives there, and I will tell you how they are sustained. They live from a stone of purest kind. It is called lapsit exillis. By the power of that stone the phoenix burns to ashes, but the ashes give him life again. Thus does the phoenix moult and change its plumage, which afterwards is bright and shining and as lovely as before. There never was a human so ill but that, if he one day see that stone, he cannot die within the week that follows. And in looks he will not fade. His appearance will stay the same, be it maid or man, as on the day he saw the stone, the same as when the best years of his life began, and though he should see the stone for two hundred years, it will never change, save that his hair might perhaps turn grey. Such power does the stone give a man that flesh and bones are at once made young again. The stone is also called the Grail.

"This very day there comes to it a message wherein lies its greatest power. Today is Good Friday, and they await there a dove, winging down from Heaven. It brings a small white wafer and leaves it on the stone. Then, shining white, the dove soars up to Heaven again. Always on Good Friday it brings to the stone what I have just told you and from that the stone derives whatever good fragrances of drink and food there are on earth, like to the perfection of Paradise. I mean all things the earth may bear. And further the stone provides whatever game lives beneath the heavens, whether it flies or runs or swims. Thus, to the knightly brotherhood, does the power of the Grail give sustenance".

Re-read this passage with the Glastonbury Zodiac in mind. Munsalvaesche, Mount of Salvation, becomes Glastonbury Tor, on the sign of the Phoenix of Aquarius. In ancient times before the precession of the equinoxes moved on, this was the period of the winter solstice, when the sun-bird died and was reborn. (Celts used a moulting and dying eagle for this bird, as the tale of the sun-god Llew in the Mabinogion shows).

The enigmatic name for the Grail-stone, "Lapsit exillis" is a typical misspelling by Wolfram from the latin, either from "lapis ex Caelis" (stone from heaven) or "lapsit e caelis" (it fell from heaven).

Wolfram's spelling was never his strong point, as he himself cheerfully admits. But his lapses nonetheless constitute a mystery. "How", Arthurian scholars debate among themselves, "could such an ignoramus compose and write such a numinous poem?". Moreover, his spelling is not uniformly bad – it is only the names of places and heroes that he trips over. Can it be that he deliberately jumbles them to preserve a secret?

His hermit mentions in this passage the two birds of the Glastonbury Zodiac, the Aquarian Phoenix and the Libran dove. The Phoenix is the Water-Carrier, alias the Celtic Cauldron of Inspiration and Rebirth – a Vessel that is usually seen as the prototype of the Grail-vessel. The dove is another symbol of renewal; a sunray descending on Good Friday, or the spring equinox, to fertilise mother Earth and awaken her dormant seed. In our Zodiac it descends from Sagittarius the sun-god's head toward Virgo, who catches it in her wheatsheaf or cornucopia. So in Christian iconography the dove is often seen flying in towards the Virgin at the Annunciation. If Christ was born at the winter Solstice, her seed was sown by the Holy Spirit at the Spring Equinox. But Wolfram may be giving another clue here by mentioning Good Friday, for the Dove of the Somerset Temple hovers over the Crucified Christ-figure concealed within the effigy of Gemini. As in the Baptism in Jordan, its message is "This is my beloved Son, in whom I am well pleased".

Virgo in our Zodiac is defined by the river Cary. Here then is Britain's first mother Goddess, Mother Cary. Virgin soil, she cares for and carries us all, "whether we fly or run or swim", as Wolfram put it. Her name is a portmanteau word which includes both caer (stone) and Ceres' corn. The Earth herself then is Wolfram's Stone. This explains another enigmatic clue of his, (also in Book 9), when he describes the Grail-Stone as "so heavy that all of sinful humanity cannot move it from its place". This is equally true of the Somerset effigy of Virgo, who is all of four miles long.

For our own sake and that of our children's children, do we not desperately need to recover this Templar vision of our dear Mother Earth, so raped and defiled now, so caring and uncared for?

I have emphasised Wolfram's secret debt to Britain and its Zodiac, but he himself paints a fairer picture of his sources. He gives Parzival a curiously pied black-and-white half-brother, Fierefiz, born to Gahmuret Parzival's father by his first wife, a Moorish princess. Thus he acknowledges the part played by astrological sages from the south and east in the European revival of Arthurian-Zodiacal matters. Flegetanis the Toledo Jew may not have existed in fact, but he symbolised the universal cosmology emerging from Europe's Moorish-inspired first university. No-one has yet found any trace of Kyot either, but he too may represent his homeland, Provence, as the place where the two sundered cosmological traditions of east and west, Arab-Chaldean and Druidic, met in the 12th century, married and produced their child-prodigy – Grail legend – which was to put all Europe in ferment.

The Crusades, at their height when Wolfram wrote Parzifal, obviously influenced him - as they did other Grail conteurs of the time. The Templars, posted for long periods in the Middle East, were profoundly affected by their enemy's culture, so superior in many ways to their own; so much so that the Church was able to accuse them of heresy. But even the Church was infected by Arab star-lore; Popes studied astrology, and Zodiacs appeared on the porches and floors of churches and cathedrals.

The Glastonbury Zodiac, as I have tried to show in my book of that name, was known to initiates in the Middle East through Cretan and Phoenician commerce with Britain from at least the time of Homer and Hesiod; probably long before, as Mrs Maltwood indicates, among the Sumerians. Traces of a far-western Paradise or Underworld appear in the Odyssey and the Theogony, and in the even earlier Epic of Gilgamesh. Greek Titans bore names of startling familiarity to us like Albion and Erin, lying turned to stone on mountain-tops in the far west. And in the Gnostic Gospel of Bartholomew Christ himself whisks that trembling saint to the west and makes him trample on the head of a fearsome giant, treading him into the earth - very much as St Padarn is said to have done to Arthur. The ancient prophecy of Melkin, already briefly mentioned, where Joseph of Arimathea lay surrounded by thirteen foretelling spheres of prophecy in Avalon, has a truly Gnostic flavour.

Wolfram's undoubtedly British Grail came to him through some such eastern source. Perhaps this accounts for the distorted Utepandragun and Famorgan? The Jew Flegetanis may have had trouble with Celtic names, but his numinous "Grail-stone" of starry import and Solomonic wisdom, dropped to earth by angels (like the stone altars of David and Carantoc) and giving all sustenance both physical and spiritual to those who guard it, even conferring Phoenix-like immortality – surely resembles our Zodiac so closely that it can hardly refer to anything else.

ST CADVAN, c. 490, also received "a sacred altar sent by a hand from heaven", which fell to earth at Tywyn, Merioneth. "And happy was the town in possessing it", says the old record, written down about 1250.

Cadvan was a Breton prince, grandson of the Armorican king Emir Llydaw. He left with a band of young dispossessed princelings for Wales, to escape from the invasion of Clovis, according to the hagiographer Rees.

By now we are not surprised to read of royal saints with these heavenly handouts; but what is new is to find one in Merioneth. It was called "the Glory of Merioneth", and Cadvan's biographer adds that "it was furnished like David's, so it is not right to pass over the place in silence, for its dwellings were equal to the mighty mansions of Heaven".

This "Altar" can not have been just a sacred meteorite, fallen literally from the sky; nor from its mansions does it seem like the primitive church of that time. They certainly sound like the Houses of the Zodiac.

Is there a Star-Temple like Glastonbury's, at Tywyn, forgotten now and awaiting rediscovery? Or was it Cadvan's zodiacal Druid-Christian teaching which cast such a memorable after-glow over the place?

Padarn, who certainly seems to have known of the terrestrial giant Arthur, was Cadvan's cousin, and Cunan who by his royal birth was to obtain "the Secret, know to few" in Taliesin's poem quoted earlier – was one of Cadvan's band. It is also significant that he took them to Bardsey Island, by its name a Druid stronghold, and founded a monastery. Meilyr, a bard of the 1100's, says that Bardsey was "the holy island of the Glain" (the mysterious Druid adder-stone) to which pertains a splendid representation of re-exaltation". Awkward as this translation is, it shows Bardsey as an ancient Mystery Centre. It was on this ancient tradition that Cadvan raised his monastery; it became known as the Isle of Saints, and 20000 saints are reputedly buried there.

ST PETROC, 5th - 6th century, c 504 -594.

References to the Glastonbury Zodiac in the Life of Cornwall's patron saint are so well disguised that at first reading I missed them entirely; I was disappointed, the more so because his father, Clemens Duke of Cornwall, bears the name of my own maternal Cornish family, some of whom still live in East Cornwall not far from Stoke Climsland (Clemensland) which is the traditional head-quarters of the Duchy – now of course owned by H.R.H. It couldn't be in better hands. The Clemens name may derive from Clemens Valerius Maximus (the Prince Macsen of the Welsh Mabinogion who married Helen of the Hosts, a Welsh princess).

In the Life of St Cadoc, St Petroc's nephew, Petroc is said to be the son of Glywis (you can pronounce this as Lewis) ruler of Dyfed, South Wales: and Wade-Evans, an authority on such matters, sees "Clemens" as a corruption of Glywis. However, as the Silurians reigned on both sides of the Severn, Glywis and Clemens may be one and the same name. Either way these families traced back traditionally to Anna Duchess of Cornwall and Brittany, mother of the Virgin in cherished local legend, and so were called the "Holy Families of Britain".

"Concerning the woman Anna", says the old MS no. 20 in Jesus College Oxford, "it was disclosed that she was the child of Hebrews whose dwelling place was Worthy Oak" (Holy Oak, a Druidic centre?) "and who sought their fortune in gold". It seems then that she was of the Phoenicians who came to trade in British metals and remained to rule; it has already been remarked how many early British dukes and kings had Middle-Eastern names. St Petroc himself can be equated with Peter, a middle-eastern name said to mean "stone", but really meaning a foundation-stone, a cube, four-square, for "ped" in Welsh means four.

With such antecedents then I naturally expected to find in St Petroc's legend traces of the Ancient Secret - but it was not until I had compared it with those of St Carantoc and St David and found tell-tale similarities that they began to emerge.

Two Lives of this saint are preserved in the National Library of Paris, their gaps helped out by an abridgement made by John of Tynemouth; my immediate source is Canon Doble's Lives of the Cornish Saints.

Though a prince, Petroc chose to abandon worldly glory, "setting his heart on a heavenly kingdom". Taking sixty willing nobles with him, he sailed to Ireland where they studied "divine rather than human letters" for twenty years. (Druids are said to have had to study for the same length of time, and as in Petroc's time there could hardly have been enough Christian literature available to keep them occupied for so long one imagines they imbibed a good deal of Druidic teachings too - perhaps in a Druidic college lately converted to Christ.

This suspicion is confirmed, for when they sailed for Cornwall "rejoicing soberly in the special gift of knowledge and fullness of learning he had attained", Petroc performs a very Druidic miracle: he causes a spring to well up for the benefit of some thirsty peasants of Trebetherick (Petroc's place). I suspect the Druids had taught him to dowse for water. They send him to St Samson nearby at Lelissick, and so anxious is Petroc to converse with this holy man that Samson is struck rigid, to make sure that he is not out when Petroc calls. Luckily this wears off as soon as greetings are exchanged. Samson (not surprisingly perhaps) soon sends him to St Wethinoc at Landewednack (Wethinoc's chapel). Petroc asks if they can all live with him, but Wethinoc and his monks hastily move out to make room for the noble band of sixty, "rejoicing that he had been worthy to prepare a place of habitation for the man of God". (Perhaps he feared being struck paralytic too?) "Blessed Petroc entered the cell with his disciples, and there for thirty years he lived, and led so innocent a life that he did to none what he would not have done to himself". But what he did to himself was awful; it gives an interesting insight into the way of life of these holy men. "He so afflicted his body with vigils and endurance of cold that, to repress the unlawful motions of concupiscence, he often plunged himself into the middle of a torrent and stood naked there from cockcrow till dawn: though indeed he practised such great frugality as was sufficient of itself to conquer the longings of the flesh". He ate bread only, except on Sundays when he took a little pulse. But on fast-days he mixed his bread with ashes.

Stranger still, when he had set his monks to make a mill for his monastery, "he is said to have carried on his shoulders morning and evening a stone of great size, in memory of which thing the same stone is preserved and placed on his tomb, and to this day scrapings from it mixed with water confer prompt remedy on the faithful who are sick". Masochism apart, why should Petroc carry the same stone each day when there were so many stones to be carried in the making of monastery and mill? There is something odd about this memory.

It might of course simply be a pun upon his name; there are several saints' tales that seem to have arisen that way - St Kea with his barge which unmoored itself from the quay to follow him; St Wino, a hairy hermit chiefly remembered for having got mad drunk on a single glass of wine - an indulgence to which he was totally unused. But Petroc with a millstone about his neck could be an echo of David's and Carantoc's "stone altars". His further adventures deepen suspicion.

After the obligatory pilgrimage to Rome (with which later Roman monkish chroniclers credited many Celtic saints, whether they actually went there or not), Petroc visited Jerusalem's holy places and then set out "for the furthest bounds of India". Here, overcome by fatigue, he fell asleep on its shore. "Awakening, the servant of God saw a vessel borne towards him on the sea, full of light within, large enough to hold only one man. Beholding the vessel which the clemency of the Almighty had prepared for him, he confidently entered it and was wafted across the sea without oar or rower, and joyfully reached a certain island. Here for seven years he led a contemplative life in the company of holy men he found there, nourished only by a single fish placed before him from time to time by the divine will at suitable hours". This suspicious fish remained whole and entire at the end of the seven years. An angel then appeared in his sleep, telling Petroc to embark in the same vessel until he came to the shores of western Britain, where he would find a staff he had left with a sheepskin, guarded by a wolf which the Lord had prepared for him as a companion on his journeying.

Arrived in "western Britain" - which I suspect Petroc had never left - he found that "There reigned at that time Teudur, a cruel and fierce man who to punish criminals had with savage ferocity caused various serpents and noxious worms to be collected in a marshy lake". At his death his son, who succeeded him, "forbade this torment to be inflicted upon men, and the hungry reptiles turned and destroyed each other by frequent attacks with livid tooth", so that at last only one remained - a horrible monster of enormous size who tore to pieces cattle and men with his savage jaws.

When news of this peril reached the man of God, he boldly approached the monster, determined to conquer him, armed with the invincible shield of faith, in conjunction with Wethinoc and Samson. He bound him with a handkerchief and was leading him to the sea when he met a party of 300 men carrying, amid lamentations, the lifeless body of a prince's son, to fulfil the rites of burial according to the custom of the country. Terrified at the sight of this most hideous monster, some fell prostrate to the ground like dead men; others, trembling as they stood, were hardly able to carry the bier. Petroc, taking pity on the mourners, kneeled and prayed; and having implored the clemency of the Almighty, restored to all their strength and raised to life again the young man whom they had borne as a corpse. Then, while they were rejoicing in the praises of God, the saint commanded the monster, which he had bound, to hurt no-one any more and to depart to solitude beyond the seas:. He then took twelve of his eighty monks and went to live in the wilderness, "among the hollows of mountains, in hiding-places of the rocks". Here he again strikes a rock with his staff and causes a fountain of pure water to spring up, as they found the wilderness in short supply.

It was the binding of the Zodiacal monster with his handkerchief that clinched it for me. The Gotha Life gives it as a stole, exactly as in the Life of St Carantoc. The marshy lake in which the tyrant Teudur had collected these monsters was none other than the marshy Vale of Avalon!

I was reminded of Arthur's dream before the fatal battle of Camlann - a striking picture of Arthur as Sagittarius upside-down on the Zodiac's Wheel, to be found at the end of Malory's Morte D'Arthur. "King Arthur dreamed a wonderful dream .... him seemed he sat upon a chaflet in a chair, fast to a wheel, in the richest cloth of gold that might be made; and the king thought there was under him, far from him, an hideous deep black water, and therein were all manner of serpents and worms and wild beasts, foul and horrible. And suddenly the king thought the wheel turned up-so-down, and he fell among the serpents, and every beast took him by a limb...". (Capricorn has one of his legs, Scorpio menaces him with claws and sting, the serpent-headed Whale in Pisces mangles his arm at Wallyer's Bridge).

In earlier versions it is said to be the Wheel of Fate, and the Fate-goddess herself ceases to smile upon him, frowns and gives her wheel a turn that brings him down. It is an extraordinary piece of design that those Zodiac signs involved in Arthur's downfall are only those ruled by Mars, Saturn and Pluto – astrology's "malefic" planets. And as the Zodiac of Glastonbury is the original Round Table, and Rhys ap Tudor is said in old records to have brought the Round Table to Wales in 1087 from Brittany, it is intriguing, to say the least, to find an earlier Tudor in Celtic Britain as its owner. Tudors seem to have inherited its royal secret; it would be more accurate to say that Rhys ap Tudor brought the *knowledge* of the Round Table back to Britain in 1087 from Brittany, whence his ancestor had taken it centuries before.

But Gawain too, in the "Quest of the Holy Grail" (written c1225) dreamed of the Round Table as a rack in a meadow that fed 150 bulls. This certainly resembles a round tract of land – like the Zodiac – not a literal table. Our Zodiac, though long forgotten, seems to be embedded in the Celtic collective unconscious, from which dreams arise.

The monster reptile tamed by Petroc (and in turn by Carantoc) must be the Whale of Pisces whose jaws extend into a serpent's neck and open jaws; a real Loch Ness Monster. So it is significant that leading it seaward Petroc encountered the dead Prince and his mourners – the dying young Son of the Sun, of Gemini's Dundon and Lollover hills! I was once told of the Dirge-singers of Dundon by a past Zodiac researcher, now dead, but have never been able to find any evidence for them until now. This legend of Petroc is a possible clue to their existence in a dim pagan past. If it was a Druidic-Phoenician rite, such mourners are by no means improbable; Phoenicians annually mourned with extravagant intensity in spring their beautiful, young and dying Adonis-Eshmun, or Iesu-Munu. And Petroc indeed brought him back to life as the Jesus of Christianity.

After this triumph, Petroc significantly takes twelve monks with him to hide away as hermits in hill-hollows and rock-clefts. Is this not a hint at the Zodiac?

The Vita Petroci has several other legends, including another pathetic dragon-patient from whose eye Petroc extracted a painful splinter, perhaps the constellation Draco. But let us examine the tales so far given, beginning with Petroc asleep on India's far shore.

"India" and "Chaldea" appear to be code-names in Celtic and Arthurian legend for star-lore – "the Mysteries of the East". Lolling-headed Gemini, asleep on the sea-shore or in his moored Cancerian moon-boat recurs so frequently in sun-myth that Petroc is in distinguished company, especially when we see this same luminous vessel approaching to waft him westwards. (One commentator on this legend actually assumed that this vessel was the moon in which "absurdly" Petroc was said to have travelled. But he wrote before this Zodiac was discovered.) Noting that there was only room for one man in the moon-boat, I doubt very much whether Petroc needed to leave the shore of Somerset at all; Severn Sea often washed right up to Dundon, and Gemini fits his boat as snugly as an acorn it its cup. Nor need the saint have gone to Jerusalem - for the concept of Glastonbury as the New Jerusalem has I suspect been with us ever since St David's sapphire altar fell to his feet from the skies, a shrine "in which the body of Our Lord once lay", and sent by air-mail from the Patriarch of the Heavenly City. As has already been observed, there are many correspondences between the Heavenly City and the Zodiac in St John's Revelations, and elsewhere. Of course there are, for both are microcosmic reflections of the Macrocosmos.

The Certain Island that Petroc eventually reached in his lunar vessel is also, one suspects, the Isle of Avalon; for he was fed for seven years by the Salmon of Wisdom – obligatory diet for so many Celtic saints – the Fish of Wearyall Hill. This Fish in Celtic myth swam up and down the Severn rescuing the Mabon (who I have learnt to see as Gemini) from his prison of Oeth and Anoeth, the Charnel-House of Bones. The wisdom of this salmon can free Man from his bondage to the flesh.

It was this ancient astrological system of self-knowledge that Petroc was acquiring, not so much asleep as contemplating his navel, with the help of the Fish and the holy men (Druids, Druid-Christians, or even perhaps the twelve Signs of Avalon's Zodiac) in his seven-year sojourn on that island. The Gotha Life of St Petroc adds that it seemed to him that he was in Paradise - and so he was; the place-name Paradise occurs twice on this "island"; three times if one counts the old farm named Heaven's Gate near the Guard-Dog's tail.

But what about the noisome reptile-infested lake, Teudur's punishment-block, the Hell of Arthur's dream? Or Hellard Hill, Hellyar's Farm, Helland, all on or near the Dog Cerberus, Guardian of this Celtic Hades? The contradiction is more apparent than real, for this is the Celts' Annwn, both Hell and Paradise, where the ancient wisdom-system taught that we get what we deserve.

When our saint's seven-year apprenticeship was over (seven steps or notes to the octave of perfection, as cut on the Tor's steep slopes - an essential part of these ancient teachings), Petroc is told by an angel to sail in the same vessel to western Britain, where he will find a staff he had left with a sheepskin, guarded by a wolf, destined to be his companion. Are these not the mast of his ship near Aries' fleece, and the Guardian Dog himself?". And / or Leo? Both Dog and Lion lie near Gemini, and both appear in Arthurian myth as guides or helpers to Grail-Questing knights. Perceval acquired a lion; various knights followed the Questing Beast (called also the Glasting Beast in Malory) by sound if not by sight, for she had twelve baying pups in her belly. This is drawn by the Parrett river, also noisy at its spring-tide bore. It was the rumour of her 12 hidden pup-signs that drew Grail-Questers to her.

Though chiefly remembered at Padstow and Bodmin now, Petroc is a pan-Celtic saint with dedications in Wales, Somerset, Devon and Brittany. His "absurd" legends indicate, as I hope to have shown, that he too learnt and taught the Zodiac mysteries, infusing them into early Celtic Christianity. He was always kind to dragons!

12th century stone carving at Kilpeck
Hereford

9th cent. Saint with bell and crozier, White Island
Co. Fermanagh, Ireland

CHAPTER 5

THE HOLY BOY

Several young Celtic saints, usually royal, survived efforts by jealous rivals to drown them at birth by putting them to the mercy of the waves in a barrel or coracle (like Danae and Perseus, or Semele and Dionysus). However real these saints may have been, there is no doubt that this particular adventure is sun-myth, pinned on them by admirers still imbued with Druid parables.

In Druidic times, says Morien Morgan in "The Mabyn of the Mabinogion", an effigy babe was put out to sea or lake in a coracle and returned, sunlike, in a new body supposed to have been made for him during his passage under the earth by the goddess Ceridwen. This annual solar drama he tells us appears to have been performed in many places in Britain and Ireland by the "Mabinogion", or Adherents of the Babe Sun. But of this, more will appear in the chapter on St Mabyn.

ST BUDOC, c 600, remembered at St Budeaux, Plymouth, is really a Breton saint. His mother, the beautiful Azenor, was daughter to Goello, Count of Brest. She saved his life when a serpent fastened itself on his arm by anointing her breast with oil and milk, so that the serpent sprang at her instead. She then cut off the poisoned breast and flung it with the serpent still attached into the fire. But God healed her, giving her a golden breast instead. (Has her native town's name generated this tale, or vice versa?).

Her mother died and the Count married again; but the new stepmother, jealous of Azenor's beauty, accused her falsely of infidelity to her husband, and she was put into a cask and thrown into the sea, vainly protesting her innocence. St Brigit, the "Mary of the Gaels", however, sent an angel to comfort and feed her - presumably through the bung-hole. In these cramped quarters her baby was born, and as soon as she had made the sign of the cross over him he spoke, prophesying that their woes would soon come to an end. (Taliesin also prophesied at birth.). Soon their barrel landed at Beauport, Ireland; a villager hoping for free wine was just about to drive his gimlet into it when he heard the babe within warning him to take care. Shocked, he ran to tell a priest, who didn't believe him until the man protested "Would I be here now, your reverence, if there'd be anything to drink in it?" This was convincing; the priest hastened to the shore and released the prisoners. The child grew up in the local abbey school while his noble mother took in washing for a living.

Meanwhile the wicked step-mother confessed on her death-bed, and the penitent Count searched the high seas for his lost daughter; though he found her at last, constant sea-sickness had undermined his health (her stomach it seems was stronger than his) and he died in her arms. Azenor also died in Ireland.

Budoc, now a monk, was because of his noble birth thus revealed, made abbot of Beau Port Abbey, and later archbishop and even king of that district. But after two years, despairing of his "barbarous flock" (his chauvinist Breton hagiographer assures us) he sailed for Brittany in a stone coffin and was promptly made archbishop of Dol. Is this, one wonders, a variation on the stone altars which floated other saints over the sea?

He visits Pope Gregory the Great, which gives us an approximate date for his life. After twenty years of unblemished sanctity, details not recorded, he dies with an odd bequest; instructing a monk called Hydultus to cut off his right arm and take it to Plourin, a token of forgiveness for their attempt to kill him for trying to curb their hideous vices. This relic is still there, says Albert le Grand, in a silver reliquary placed on Budoc's stone coffin, and punishes those who dare to swear false oaths upon it.

In view of Budoc's early identification with the Zodiac Babe in the Boat, I am suspicious about this right arm; it is one of Gemini's unusual characteristics, and features in St Collen's fight with the oddly-named Giant Bras. Is the name Hydultus a clue to Glastonbury's Twelve Hides, the Hidden Figures? And whatever happened to Azenor's husband? Shouldn't he have sought for her too? He is strangely absent from the tale. But if this is sun-myth, the sun is the father of the waif cast out upon the waves, and Azenor's is a sort of implied Virgin-Birth, not too explicitly stated, for we are now 600 years into Christianity. The births of St David and St Mungo are also perilously heretical.

Perhaps it is not so surprising then to find that Glastonbury Abbey in the 1300's had a relic of St Budoc.

Zennor in Cornwall takes its name from Azenor.

ST DECUMAN, Patron of Watchet, on the Somerset coast near Minehead, was one of the many saints who sailed across the Severn estuary on unlikely vessels; his was a hurdle. He lived alone in a cell sustained only by a cow, and was murdered by brigands. His chief claim to distinction is that when his head was cut off, he walked with it under his arm to his well! But as he is claimed as Arthur's bishop, and as Gemini's lolling head tends to be decapitated, there is reason to see him as yet another

Holy Boy of Somerset's Zodiac with his Taurean cow. There is also a farm called Kentchurch only half a mile away whose name hagiographers identify with St Keyne, a saint who shows every sign of being the Virgin Mother-Goddess. Decuman is sculptured on the west front of Wells Cathedral, holding his head, and his Day was made much of at Muchelney Abbey, where it was a principle feast. Both places are very near the Zodiac. He had chapels near Brecon (Llandegyman, Llanvihangel) and at Wendron in Cornwall, so though so little is known of him now, he was once widely feted in the west. He is said to have been martyred in the year 706.

ST KENTIGERN or MUNGO, Glasgow's patron saint, was another divinely-fathered Boy at the mercy of the waves even before birth. His mother Themis or Thaney, found herself miraculously with child. Her father king Lot of Lothian had married Arthur's sister Morgause and produced Gawain, Gareth and Gaheris, all Round Table knights, so Thaney was their sister. The Arthurian connection is significant, as is Clydeside where Kentigern is best remembered, for it was a Druid refuge long after the coming of Christianity. Merlin or Merddin, banished to Strathclyde, bemoaned the loss of Somerset's Secrets in his poem "Avallenau" (apple trees) in the 6th century.

Lot didn't believe his daughter's miracle, and furious, had her thrown from Traprain Law, a high cliff; but she was miraculously uninjured, so he next cast her adrift in an oarless coracle on the Firth of Forth. However, she landed safe at Culross in Fife, where her child was born, and both were revived by a fire left by shepherds. (Shepherds often attend a sun-king's birth).

They were found and cared for by Servan, a kindly monk. When the boy Kentigern grew, he educated him in his school, and showed him great favour, calling him Mungo, "dear friend". This aroused the other boys' jealousy, so they killed Servan's pet robin and blamed it on Kentigern. But the little saint prayed and brought it back to life. (Robins from their red breasts were solar symbols. "Who killed Cock Robin?" is said to be a dirge for the dying sun). Kentigern, having fallen from a cliff and risen from the water, was a symbol of solar death and resurrection too, as this little episode no doubt emphasises.

In 550, now a trained monk, he left Servan to visit Fergus, a holy man at Kernach. Fergus had been told that he would not die until he had seen the man who was destined to convert the whole district to Christianity. As this was Kentigern, his visit was fatal. Kentigern put Fergus' body on a cart drawn by two wild bulls and let them take it where they would, Celtic fashion, and buried it where they stopped, raising a church over it. This later grew into Glasgow Cathedral, one of the many Celtic foundations whose site was chosen by animals.

Kentigern is always portrayed with a salmon and a ring, due to the following miracle. King Roderick gave his queen a precious ring, one always handed down from royal father to son; but she gave her heart and the ring with it to a knight at court. While he slept by the river the king passing by saw it on his finger, drew it off stealthily and flung it in the river, then asked his wife why she was not wearing it. She at once asked her lover for it, and finding it gone went distracted with fear to kindly St Kentigern for help. He, perhaps remembering his mother, had a soft spot for fallen women; he prayed, then went angling and fished up a salmon which proved to have the precious ring in its belly. Thus the queen was able to wear it again and whatever the king's private opinion, made it impossible for him to arraign her publicly.

This story is told of other saints, among them St Asaph, when the ring was traditionally one always worn by queens of Wales. May it not be the royal secret of the Zodiac circle which belongs to the Earth-Mother? And is the salmon not the Celtic Salmon of Wisdom, transported from the Severn to the Clyde with Merddyn? The 12th century MS in the British Museum records that Kentigern blessed the hairy Lailoken–Merddyn. In yet another version Lailoken spilt the beans by accusing the queen of adultery and was murdered at her instigation.

Kentigern is thus inextricably bound up with Arthurian – hence Zodiacal – myth. His last episode therefore takes on deeper significance than might at first appear. Feeling in old age his death approaching, he ordered a hot bath – and died in it, signing himself with the cross. Some of his weeping monks prayed to be allowed to follow him, and with his last breath he promised heaven to any who stepped into his bath after him; several did and died at once.

It would be frivolous to wonder if the water was perhaps too hot? And though Cleanliness we know is next to Godliness, wasn't this taking things to extremes? Either way, it is a strange story. But after a baffled interval, a vision of the death of Llew the sun-god in the Mabinogion rose before my eyes. Llew could only be killed at one time in the year, when he took his annual bath, which he did in weird fashion by stepping into it from a goat's back. We are at the winter solstice, the sun's weakest hour, stepping from Capricorn into the Water-pot of Aquarius, which is also the Celtic Cauldron (always on the boil) of rebirth and inspiration. At this moment Llew's rival pierced him with a spear which had been a whole year in the making, and that only when all good people were in church. Llew's spirit left him with a great cry, flying up into the sky in the form of an eagle. The Glastonbury Aquarius is also an eagle or phoenix – both birds being crested symbols of rebirth.

Kentigern the Christian was demonstrating that just as the sun dies at the winter solstice and is gloriously resurrected, so it is with human souls. His day is January the 14th, surely no accident.

And was it accident merely that at the time of writing this I went to Ravenna, there to see among other wonders the tomb of Theodoric the Goth, the 5th - 6th century conqueror of Rome? For to my astonishment his sarcophagus was undeniably in the form of a portable bath, though fashioned in extremely unportable red phorphyry, so weighty that it must have needed an army to raise it into position, for it stands alone in a domed vault on the upper floor of his two-storeyed mausoleum. Two handles, carved immovably on its sides, were reminiscent of the real handles of baths still in use in my childhood, when bathrooms were rare. A lion's head carved on one side proclaimed not only a conqueror but a sun-king; for the sun rules Leo's royal sign. (Llew is also Leo.)

Was blood-red porphyry chosen to infuse new life into the royal corpse? The timing of this discovery was astonishing in more than one way - for Theodoric and Kentigern lived in much the same period.

But Theodoric the Ostrogoth and Kentigern the western Scot, both dying in the sun-king's bath? Not so impossible, for Theodoric was at least nominally subject to Byzantium, and thus heir by adoption to eastern calendrical and Zodiacal traditions; while Kentigern inherited the same, once universal, ideas from the Druids.

ST MELOR is another young son-of-the-sun of ancient times who has become a youthful saint, indeed a martyr. He is the patron saint of Amesbury only two miles from Stonehenge, which was one of the Three Perpetual Choirs of Druidic Britain, known even in Greece of the 6th century BC, where Hecateus described it as a "magnificent grove of Apollo, and a remarkable temple, of a round form, adorned with many consecrated gifts. There is also a city sacred to the same god, most of whose inhabitants are harpers, who continually play upon their harps in the temple and sing hymns to the god, extolling his actions". He also says that Apollo visited the temple every nineteen years to celebrate the Metonic cycle of sun and moon, which further identifies his temple as Stonehenge, where this cycle is marked by the 56 Aubrey holes. Amesbury then was the "city" of Druidic harpers and singers recorded in the Cymric Triads as one of three

"Perpetual Choirs". Apollo Maleatas the Apple-god was known here as Avallach. Amesbury, (Ambresbyrig in 883) seems to derive from Greek Ambrosios - Divine.

It is not surprising then to find a saint with such marked sun-god characteristics at Amesbury. It was to Amesbury's nunnery that Guinevere retired after Arthur's passing; here she took a tragic farewell of her lover Lancelot, who then went to become a penitent monk at Glastonbury.

If Lancelot is the Lance of Light - the summer sun - he was travelling west to his setting; taking the same route that his king had travelled in his funeral barge to Avalon's Apple-Isle before him, sailing from the edge of Salisbury plain down the river Brue and being buried on the sunset line of Glastonbury Abbey's nave. Glastonbury and Stonehenge are connected not only mythically but geomantically. Is it accident merely that a queen survives in Amesbury church's mediaeval glass? For here the queen of the earth bids farewell to her lover the sun. Arthurian myth is Druidic sun-myth preserved and transmuted into Christianity.

St Melor's story confirms this. His wicked uncle Rivaldus had killed his father Melianus, Rivaldus' own brother, in order to gain the throne of Brittany, and had designs on the life of Melor too, but he was too popular and Rivaldus too unpopular for him to dare to kill his saintly little nephew outright. He did, however, persuade his subjects to maim him, thus rendering him unfit to reign, by cutting off one hand and one foot. A cunning smith, however, made Melor a silver hand and a bronze foot, which not only fitted (no rejection problems) but grew in proportion with the lad's growth and were able to be used like normal limbs. This, of course, puts him at once in the Celtic sun-king class of Nuada and Lugh, who both had silver hands.

Seeing that Melor grew in grace and in his subjects' love, Rivaldus then tried to poison him secretly – but the child, divinely omniscient, made the sign of the cross over the food and the poison became apparent to all. Needless to say he pardoned his poisoners freely with Christlike generosity.

As it was clear that he was in grave danger, Melor fled to the castle of his relative Count Commorus, but Rivaldus had bribed his erstwhile guardian and tutor Kyoltan to slay him secretly and bring the head to him as evidence, promising him all the land he could see from Cornubia's highest hill. Kyoltan wormed his way into the castle with a show of love for his pupil and cut off Melor's head while he slept, putting it all bloodstained as it was into a leather bag. But on the way to Rivaldus the head became heavier and heavier, until Kyoltan was exhausted and lay down, unable to carry it further. Then the head, ever-compassionate to enemies, spoke, advising the murderer to kick a nearby rock, which would then pour forth a spring of water. Kyolton, much refreshed by this miracle of mercy completed his journey, showed the head, and climbing the mountain to survey his promised land – was immediately struck blind so he could see nothing at all. He died shortly after, overcome by his own guilty conscience. Rivaldus too died very satisfactorily in horrible agonies.

Melor is honoured in Cornwall at Mylor, Merther Mylor and Linkinhorne, and at many more places in Brittany, from whence his cult came to Amesbury. The itinerant Breton monks who brought his relics there (it is thought in the 900's) never meant them to stay, but when they tried to take them from the altar they were found to be stuck immovably. The little sun-king obviously felt at home there, for reasons already conjectured. But it is from Brittany that the fullest and most circumstantial accounts are derived, giving names and incidents which seem to identify him with what I believe to be his original, the Gemini Boy of Somerset.

Melor's father Melianus (or Meliavus) has a name closely resembling Meliodas, Sir Tristram's father, and Count Commorus who sheltered Melor, is very like King Mark of Cornwall who is "Quonomorus" on an inscribed Celtic stone. But Tristram "the sad god" has many points of identification with Gemini, being for instance too young for knighthood when he defeats Sir Marhaus, thus saving the Cornish from Irish bondage. And we have already noted the seasonal element in his summer abduction of Isolde, the wife of wintry King Mark. Kyoltan is probably the same assassin as Sir Kay, who decapitated Arthur's young son Lohot .When he showed their son's head to Arthur and Guinevere *two* suns shone at once through the windows of Arthur's hall.

One incident in Melor's life which recalls Gemini lying invisible on his hill occurs when the boy, fleeing over a hill at Lanmeur from Rivaldus, prays for help; the earth miraculously opens, making a shallow depression in which he lies. The horsemen pursuing him leap right over him without seeing him, and Melor is temporarily saved. Another happens after his decapitated head has been brought to Rivaldus; his body will not stay buried but keeps on appearing on the surface until the head, drawn on a carriage by bulls, is brought to be buried with it. The two adjacent hills of Dundon and Lollover may well be the origin of this strange tale, for Taurus the bull overlooks them from the north. And may the size of Dundon Hill not account for the ever-growing weight of Melor's head?

Melor, though a Breton saint, was remembered as being of British blood; his ancestor Daniel, son of John, Duke of Cornwall, succeeding to the throne of Brittany in 670. These names are notably Hebrew or Phoenician, as are several in these western royal families, and help to fuel the suspicion that Melor is a variant of Amalek or Avallach, a Phoenician-Druid sun-god from pre-Christian times. But as this possibility has already been discussed at the end of chapter one, to avoid repetition I will refer the reader back to that chapter.

Melor's mother Aurilla was also British, being the daughter of Count Judoc - an equally Jewish or Phoenician name - of Devon. It is interesting to find one Judhael possessing Totnes Castle after the Conquest; no doubt he was among William the Conqueror's Breton contingent, thirsting to regain his ancient domain, lost for some centuries to the Saxon invaders.

ST CENYYDD (KENETH). About 1320 John of Tynemouth found this strange story in Wales. The saint seems entirely mythical, but none the less interesting to Zodiac researchers for that. For here in St Keneth we have I believe a memory of the Gemini Babe of the Glastonbury Zodiac.

In the days of King Arthur, a Breton prince named Dihoc became the father of a child by incest. But before it was born he was summoned as a tributary to Arthur's court in Goir for Christmas, and took the woman with him. (Whether she was his daughter, mother or sister, we are not told). Keneth was thus born in Arthur's court. But he was born severely crippled – his calf adhered to his thigh.

His father ordered him to be thrown into the river, so an osier cradle was made for him and he was launched on the river Lothur and swept out to sea. A storm blew him to the isle of Inisweryn, where, cast up on the shore, seagulls swooped down in a cloud and bore him up to the rocky ledge, making a nest of breast-feathers for him and sheltering him from wind and rain with their wings. Before nine days passed, an angel descended from heaven with a brazen bell, giving him the handle to suck until an obliging doe daily spurted her milk into it from the cliff-top with unerring aim. He grew, and his baby-clothes expanded with him.

He was found one day by a local peasant who was childless and took him home, where his wife put him to bed; but the gulls who loved him swooped down on the peasant's cattle and drove them seawards; they also created havoc in his house. This was too much for the poor man, who at once carried Keneth back to his ledge – whereupon the gulls drove back the cattle and even tidied the house for him.

Until he was eighteen he lived thus, daily instructed by an angel in sacred matters, when he was told he must walk a mile to a reedy spot where he must build himself a wattle hut. He made slow progress (hardly surprising considering his disability) and to refresh himself frequently, made twenty-four springs flow in that painful mile. Here he was joined by a man who offered to be his servant, but who forswore himself on the bosom-shaped bell and at once went mad, rushed away and lived like a wild beast covered with hair until Keneth after seven years prayed for his return in his right mind. (The man had stolen a spear belonging to some robbers who St Keneth was politely entertaining and swore on the bell that he hadn't seen the spear).

Morgan, prince of Glamorgan, had gathered much plunder from an expedition and Keneth sent his man with the Bosom-bell for a share of the spoils. This was rudely refused, but as the plunderers then fell to fighting over the distribution and many were killed, Morgan belatedly offered the saint whatever he asked, fearing that worse might befall if he didn't compensate Keneth, and taking him on to a hill made the view over to him for ever.

Soon after, David, Teilo and Padarn called on Keneth to invite him to the Synod of Llandevi Brevi. "How can a cripple like me travel?" he protested; so David prayed and Keneth's leg straightened at once. But our saint was not pleased; He prayed in his turn and up went the leg as before, the calf adhering to the thigh. And there the strange story ends.

To be born at Christmas, illegitimately or by incest, and to be thrown to the mercy of the waves in infancy are all typical of young sun-gods. Incest is characteristic of Zodiac-based tales, as there is only one female figure there who has to be all women in one. Arthur himself committed incest with his sister Morgause, thus producing his Nemesis, the Scorpionic Mordred; though in Arthur's defence it must be urged that as a solar waif himself, torn from his royal mother at birth, he had no idea that the beautiful wife of King Lot was in fact his sister.

Arthur's court at Goir is often taken to be Gower - but interestingly enough, Loomis and other authorities place it in the "Summer Country" of Somerset, for Goir or Goirre in Arthurian legend has various features like a Perilous Bridge leading to a water-girdled Glass Castle, which identify it with Glastonbury. And Avalon has always been an Arthurian centre, while Gower has not.

An infant sun-god, whose leg is doubled beneath him - who can St Keneth be but Gemini in our Zodiac?

The sea-gulls who rescued and nourished him may well duplicate the Libran Dove who hovers above him, and the obliging doe who aimed her milk into his bell-cup may be Capricorn – who as the she-goat Amalthea suckled the infant Zeus in his Christmas cave, and was translated to the stars of Capricorn for her devotion. The "titty-bell" could be the bell on Taurus' neck which overhangs the Geminian effigy, and features in St David's legend, lifted from earlier Celtic myth. And is the Isle of Inis-Weryn where Keneth was washed up not Inis Wytryn, "Glass Island" - the Celtic name for Glastonbury?

I suspect that Keneth's tale was taken to Glamorgan and Gower by Celts fleeing across the Severn from victorious Saxons, and localised there, sanctifying him eventually as a Christian saint.

There *was* a historical St Cenydd who was active in Glamorgan, c 500, founding churches there; but he was the son of the perfectly respectable historian St Gildas. The mountainous Hundred of Senghenydd north of Caerphilly is supposed to be named after him. But legends live long amid the mountains; may it not be that the legends of the crippled Babe were grafted on to Gildas' son of the same name, so that he could still be revered in these fastnesses without taint of paganism?

I wonder, because by a strange coincidence, the very day after I first came across Keneth's tale in Baring Gould's Lives of the Saints, I went to take part in a Festival at Cardiff, and found to my astonishment that I had been allotted a room in the University's Senghenydd House! Is Keneth (Cennydd) not the Cenn Cruach (Bowed One of the Mound), the idol St Patrick baptised, and whom Mrs Maltwood identified with her Zodiac Gemini?

ST FFILI (Latin Filius, a son) was the son of St Cenydd, and grandson of St Gildas, our earliest historian. He had a church near his father at Rhos Ffili, and is thought to have named Caerphilly, near his father's Hundred of Senghenydd. But nothing seems to be known of him, and I believe him to be one with St Keneth, one of whose titles as Gemini in his boat must have been Son of the Sun. Ffili has no festival in the Welsh Calendar.

There is, however, an amusing anecdote surviving about his grandfather Gildas involving a boat in Brittany.

One day four devils disguised as monks came to Ruys to summon St Gildas to see their master, Philibert, who they said was dying. Gildas, though warned of them by a vision, could hardly refuse the last rites, so accompanied them in their boat but insisted that as they sailed all should sing the office of Prime. "But there is no time for that", the devils objected, "we must make all haste to find him alive". Gildas nonetheless began intoning – and the boat and crew disappeared at once, leaving him floundering in the water. However, he continued to sing, sat on part of his cloak and tying the rest to his staff for a sail, safely reached the isle of

Noirmoutier, where needless to say, he found Philibert in excellent health.

Baring-Gould objects that St Philibert was not born until after Gildas' death, and so assumes that it was his own grandson Ffili that Gildas was visiting. Baring-Gould with refreshing common-sense surmises that the sailor-monks were incompetent and overturned the boat, whereupon Gildas, known for his irascibility, used some strong language about them when he had struggled ashore. The epithet "devils!" stuck ....

I also, but for different reasons, think that the tale refers to Ffili - the Gemini Boy in the Boat. I am helped to this conclusion by the Book of Dr John David Rhys (16th century Peniarth MS 118) which gives accounts of Giants and their haunts. He tells us "Some say that Phili was a giant, a son of Bwch", (he-goat), "and had his residence at Caerphilly". Born at Capricorn's Winter Solstice? Ffili is faintly remembered in Cornwall at Philleigh near Gerrans Bay, Falmouth (Eccles. St. Filii de Eglosrhos in 1384). This is the territory of a dynasty of Gereints, brave knights of Arthur and patrons of the Celtic saints. His name at least if not his memory may also survive at Lamphil on the Camel river west of Bodmin Moor, in the parish of St Breward. Here is Slaughter Bridge (which the Cornish say was the site of Arthur's last Battle of Camlann), Arthur's Hall, many prehistoric remains and stone circles. Ffili-Keneth-Gemini, son of the dying sun-king, should be remembered there.

Only five miles away is Saint Mabyn's church; Mabon son of Modron, is another name for the same divine youth – Son of the Mother. (At Penzance is Madron church with its once-famous healing well, dedicated to St Maternas who, though now male, must once have been the ancient Modron, for you can hardly get more maternal than that).

ST EVAL or UFELWY, another son of Gildas' St Cennydd and brother of Ffili, also has a name that gives him away – for efyll means Twin in Welsh. Not only his name but his situation is significant, for his parish church was built within a stone circle, though all the stones save one have been put to making the foundations of the chancel. The churchyard, however, like St Mabyn's some twelve miles to the east, remains circular. In the parish – which lies near the north coast of Cornwall, midway between Newquay and Padstow – is a farm called Raws, where there once was a chapel called Laneff, short for Llaneffal, which Baring-Gould thinks was the earliest oratory of St Eval. It would seem that the Celtic church respected the sacred circle and built outside it, but the mediaeval church, less scrupulous, built inside it, and utilised the stones for their later building.

St Eval in 1322 was St Uvellus, a Latinised form of the name; it has many variants. In the Iolo MSS. it is spelt Ufelwyn, in the Book of Llan Dav it becomes Ubelbiu, Uvelviu, etc., names which hint at the sun-god Bel. Ufel in Welsh means fire, flame, heat. He was once patron saint of Withiel nearby, but its church is now St Clement's. Baring-Gould says that both Ffili and Ufelwy have left their mark on Cornwall, but "when these brothers were there is uncertain." I suspect that they were known far earlier than Celtic Christianity, back to the time when astronomical stone circles were being set up to read the seasons by the passage of the sun, moon and stars; for the Twins of the Zodiac have been with us since the dawn of civilisation.

William of Worcester records that "St Uffald or Uffile" had many churches in Wales; he appears in the Llan Dav register as a very doubtful bishop, and is even cited as one of the bishop-abbots who met St Augustine at the famous Oak. Could it be that the Celtic bishops put forward his name as evidence that they had long familiarity with the Christlike young sun-god who would rise again? If he once had "many churches in Wales", they have long been given to other saints; one such was Llan-Ufelwyn, now St George-super-Ely in Glamorgan, while another was Bolgros, now called Belley Moor, at Madley, Herefordshire. Bol and Belley are of course Bel.

He is also remembered in Brittany as St Yhuel (which could be translated as "the sun") said to have been a hermit of Quimperlé. His 14th century statue at Rosgrande shows him as a very young man with flowing locks.

To return to St Eval, from this maze of aliases; Bodmin Moor, his area, has long been inhospitable and barren – whatever its climate may have been in the time of the prehistoric settlements with which it is strewn. Old gods, old names and legends linger long in such places; Brown Willy may be Hywil, Heilin, Heul the sun, and Brown Gelly is perhaps a variant of it, or from the god Celu (Kelly), sun consort of Ceridwen. High Willhays on Dartmoor and Yes Tor echo these; "Yes" can only be Yesse, Esse, Esus the young god who mediates between the old faith and the new, who is remembered at Essa's Bed, (a rock outside Looe), at Hessenford, and at Saltash, which was once called Esse. A silent fanfare of holy names greets the traveller as he crosses the Tamar into Saltash, and Cornwall's Lyonesse. The Tamar itself is a female name in Genesis, and redolent of Phoenician merchantmen; the geographer Ptolemy (150 AD) notes it as Tamaros.

(As Looe cherishes memories of the coming to Britain of the Phoenician tin-trader Joseph of Arimathea and his nephew Jesus, it is an open question which Jesus or Esse they remember, the Christian or pre-Christian one.)

ST ISSUI, a shadowy Celtic hermit of Patricio, remote in the Brecon Beacons, may well be Esse or Esus, Christianised. Though beloved for good works, he was nonetheless decapitated. The spring which *issued* from the spot became a place of pilgrimage, healing many. Significantly, his "mother's" stream, Nant Mair, flows nearby. Who can she be? Mary the Virgin? But I suspect an older Mother and Son were remembered here in these remote mountains. I am indebted to Rosetta Reinke (of Massachusetts!) for pointing out that the parishes of St Issui and llangenny are adjacent. The Genny in this name is Cenau, Welsh for St Keyne, virginal daughter of King Brychan of Brecon. Her hephew St Cadoc persuaded her to return to her homeland after her wanderings, and she is remembered as finally dying at Llangenny, after blessing its "great mountain" - the famous Sugarloaf.

As we shall see in her later chapter, St Keyne acquired matriarchal aspects of the older Earth-Goddess. So in view of her proximity to St Issui we may well wonder if we do not have here memories of Virgo "who has her son Ysu in her arms". The name Genny reminds us too of Arthurian Guinevere, whose son Lacheu or Lohot was also decapitated.

The recurring place-name Kelly in Cornwall is usually interpreted as "grove"; but this could be a secondary meaning of the word, derived from groves in which Celu, pronounced "Kelly", (Coelus, the Hidden or Unknown God) was worshipped. Druids driven into the westernmost parts of Britain, survived longer in the mountains of Wales and west of the Tamar's protective barrier.

Baring-Gould observes that the Celtic saints regarded themselves as successors of their bardic Order. Where the Druids lingered so did memories of Arthur, and Kelliwic in Grail legend was Arthur's Cornish court – either at Callington (originally Kelliwic) or Kelly Bray nearby. (The headquarters of the Duchy of Cornwall is still there, at Stoke Climsland.) And Arthur, like Celu, was a sky-god; his very knights deriving their names from even older Celtic deities. Lostwithiel (early form Los-Huliel) is another evocative name in this area which has been thought to mean Court of the sun - Lys Heul.

The God Esus
chopping a willow
tree

ST SULIEN is said to be the saint of Luxulian, between Lostwithiel and St Austell. Its earlier form, Lauxsolian, is said to mean Sulien's monastery - from Llocc, a shelter or refuge.

I have been able to gather very little about him save that while in Brittany, he drew a line with a stick round his field and placed four "switches" (houssines) at each corner, which miraculously kept out marauding cows. It sounds like the first electric fence. The animals were totally immobilised until he set them free; no doubt by switching off the "switches".

He is said to have joined St Cadvan's vast band of refugee monks fleeing to Britain – these immigrations went two ways once Brittany had been colonised, and the same succession problems began to arise there too; they all settled in Bardsey island off the Lleyn peninsula. But so many of Cadvan's company had solar names that one suspects it became a useful pigeon-hole for later hagiographers to put saints of whom little was known, and who were doubtless Christianised sun-gods. Sulien's name is suspiciously like Sul the Romano–British god of Bath whose flaming locks make him Sol the sun. Was he also the god of Silbury Hill, Avebury, on the Bath road? Luxulian by the same token may have been a Druidic centre of sun-worship.

ST MABYN, an unknown saint, has a church on top of a hill in Cornwall between Bodmin and Wadebridge. In 1234 this shadowy figure was male - Sancto Malbano - but by 1266 he had suffered a sex-change into the female Sancta Mabene, which indicates a crisis of identity in the minds of the church authorities of the time. St Mabyn has been thought to be one of the many daughters of 5th century Brychan king of Brecon, who had in one count at least twenty-four children, mostly saints; but the mediaeval rule in cases of uncertain identity was to consign such Celtic saints to his vast family, on the principle that he'd hardly notice one more at his capacious board. So we may wonder if some of these cuckoos in his nest were not, in fact, baptised deities from an older faith. St Keyne, I suspect, was one such, St Mabyn another.

Mabene is suspect for another reason,; her churchyard in the hill-top village that bears her name is round. This is usually taken as a sign of a previous stone circle whose stones have been used to build a later church; a device that ensured continuity of worship at the ancient sacred site. And if some of the congregation still proved too faithful to the old deity, the next step was often to change the gender of the original one, while retaining the old name, or something near enough to it, for the new saint.

These methods were often used, and in time proved effective despite some bewilderment, one imagines, on the part of the worshippers subject to such changes. But the transition was greatly helped (as I hope to show) by the essential similarity of the old beliefs to the new.

These considerations incline me to believe that the original object of worship here was the Celtic Mabon, son of Modron the great Mother, who is the hidden – almost absent – hero of the Mabinogion. In Kilhwch and Olwen, the oldest tale in the collection (8th century) he is already half-forgotten, and to find him Kilhwch must approach the Ousel of Cigwri, a bird so old that she has worn an anvil completely away by daily sharpening her beak upon it. However, she has never heard of the Mabon; but as the search-party are Arthur's messengers, she takes them to the Stag of Redynfre who is even older. (He has seen a huge oak grow from a sapling and rot away to a decayed stump). Yet he knows nothing of the Mabon either, but obligingly guides them to the Owl of Cwm Cawlwyd who is even hoarier. But although he has outlived two generations of woodland, all he can do is pass them on to "the oldest creature that is in this world, and he that has fared furthest afield" – the Eagle of Gwernabwy. This near-immortal bird is equally ignorant, however, and can only recommend them to the Salmon of Llyn Llyw, who must be the Salmon of Wisdom, for he swims up and down the Severn as far as Caer Loyw – Gloucester Castle. He, at last, knows something, reporting that he hears terrible wailing from within the castle walls that may come from the imprisoned Mabon. Cei and Bedwyr go on the salmon's back to the castle, break down the wall and free the Mabon from his age-long servitude, while Arthur's host besiege it from the front.

Though the Mabon is indescribably ancient, he is still a young hunter, needed in Kilhwch's quest because only he can control the monstrous hound Drudwyn demanded by Olwen's Giant father in return for his daughter's hand. The Mabon's was a sad life, for he was "taken when three nights old from between his mother and the wall."

Ancient he certainly is, for Roman soldiers in Britain erected several altars to him as Apollo Maponus. But he was here before they came. The old British name for Apollo was Avallach, Avalon's apple-god, as both names imply – who in later Arthurian literature was the Maimed Grail-king of Avalon's Mysteries. (Romans obligingly incorporated native gods into their rites; a sensible reversal of the adage, "When in Rome do as the Romans do.") It was politic to placate the gods of the countries they invaded. But if he was here before they came, he must be Druidic.

The Mabon in his rare appearances betrays sun-traits. As the giant Mabonagrain in Chretien de Troyes' "Erec and Enide" he fights Erec successfully until the hour of noon, after which his strength wanes, and Erec, a mere mortal, can overcome him. He is dressed in red armour, always in Celtic myth indicative of an otherworldly or solar character. His abduction at birth is shared by various sun-gods including Arthur, as is his imprisonment, though the Mabon's life-sentence is longer than usual, as these periods probably refer to the absent sun at night or in winter months. Some authorities also suggest that they are reminiscent of male initiation rites, when the youth was removed from maternal influence and shut up for a time alone. Noble young Celts (like Arthur) were often, it seems, removed from their mothers and fostered in knightly surroundings until this ceremony, and this was justified by myth; the god of youth had undergone such an ordeal before them.

Mabon means the Youth. He trained young men in bardic song, in hunting and in medicine, all activities shared by Apollo. (Mabonagrain's garden contained every healing herb known to man.) And Apollo's mother was a Hyperborean, that is, a Briton; or so said Greek Hecateus in the 6th century BC . He tells how Apollo visited a famous Round Temple here (Stonehenge?) and danced every night at nineteen-year periods, "pleased with his own successes." Is it coincidence merely that St Mabyn's churchyard was probably once an old stone circle? The Mabon is an ancient god indeed.

His prison at Caer Loyw (usually translated as Gloucester) may be the kingdom of Logres, the area east of the Severn occupied by the Lloegrians, an early Celtic tribe. Geoffrey Ashe's researches have narrowed this kingdom down to an area bounded by the rivers Severn, Somerset Axe and Parret, in earlier days, though the Welsh later used Llogres to mean all Britain east of the Severn. But this area enclosed by these three rivers contains the Somerset Zodiac exactly. Is our dejected youth, equated with Apollo-Avallach, Avalon's maimed Grail king, not Gemini?

There are other clues to confirm this suspicion. The Mabon is the only one who can handle a monster Hound, who may well be the Guardian-Dog of the Zodiac near his effigy. He is Canis Major, though his stars cannot correspond as he is outside the circle of the planisphere. The stars of Orion the great Hunter fall, however, on Gemini's effigy, and Orion's hunting-dog was Sirius the Dog-Star in Canis Major.

Also, in the Mabinogion tale of Gereint and Enid (the Welsh version of Chretien's Erec and Enide), Mabonagrain's Enchanted Garden becomes an apple orchard in a valley. Mabonagrain is no longer a giant, nor is he named, he is simply a fierce knight on a mettlesome charger who challenges Gereint for daring to sit beside his lady in a vacant chair. This sounds like the Siege Perilous at the Round Table, and the orchard in the valley surrounded by a Hedge of Mist, very like the Vale of Avalon. The hero in both versions must venture alone into this enchanted place, whose hedge is hung about with the heads of defeated knights. It is a place of initiation, with death as the penalty for failure. In Gereint's version, this awful place is in the realms of the earl Ywein, whose brother is the Mabon, for they both have the sky-god Urien for father. So with the help of Mabonagrain we can confidently assume that Gereint's unnamed apponent is the Mabon, god of youthful initiation.

Something of the nature of the old Druidic initiation-rites can be surmised from all this. Like Gemini, the Mabon is perhaps Man himself, half-animal from his earth-mother, half-divine from his sky-father, his spirit imprisoned in flesh, for Caer Loyw is elsewhere termed the prison of Oeth and Anoeth, the Charnel-House of Bones. (Oedd = ages, lifetimes; annoedd = folly, unwisdom.) It is significant that the Mabon cannot save himself, but needs heavenly Arthur and the Salmon of Wisdom to rescue him. (The wisdom of Salaman or Solomon). What better cure for lifetimes of folly?

Rhys in "Celtic Folklore" interprets oeth as Power, with anoeth as its opposite. But with the Druids, Knowledge, not force majeur, was Power; so substantially this comes to the same thing; the initiate is released by the power of divine wisdom.

Baring-Gould records three St Mabons, all obscure. One is the supposed brother of St Teilo, of Llanvabon in Wales, while another is the son of Glas ab Glassog, which sounds suspiciously like Mabon son of Glastonbury. St John Rhys concludes "it is quite possible that one or another of them is simply Apollo Maponos in Christian garb." Avallach of Avalon!

The son of Glas ab Glassog (of Glastonbury?) is called Mabon Wyn, that is, Shining or Holy Mabon. We are told he was descended from Bran the Blessed – who as Bron helped Joseph of Arimathea bring the Grail to Britain, and was dubbed the "Rich Fisher". As this is a title also borne by Babylonian Adapa the Wise, Orpheus and Buddha, it would seem that we are among the ancient Mysteries. Druidic Mysteries too, for the wounded and dying god-king Bran (an earlier Bran), in the Mabinogion is the prototype of the Grail's Maimed Fisher-King. The Great Fish Bron caught which sustained Joseph's missionary party must have been the same Salmon of Wisdom that rescued the Mabon from imprisonment at Caer Loyw.

And if "Saint" Mabon Wyn was descended from Bron then he is of the line of Grail-Keepers. But is he a descendant? For Mabon Wyn is also called the "Aged": an odd contradiction unless this perpetual Youth was regarded as coming down from a time even more ancient than the beginning of the Christian era. It may well be that the god Bran was once in myth his father, and that with his Great Mother Modron they represented the Zodiac Family Trinity.

There is always the possibility that the three "St Mabons" were real Celtic saints named after the mythical hero; but if so they failed to achieve enough distinction for their works to be recorded; their shadowy characters hardly lend conviction as to their actual existence. Besides, the Peniarth MS 118 gives one of them as "One of the Giants of Lansawyl" – in Monmouthshire, just across the Severn from our Zodiac.

I must not leave these notes on this important and pervasive figure without mention of the researches of Morien Morgan, entitled now "the Mabin of the Mabinogion". His conclusions, written about 1900, well before the Glastonbury Zodiac was discovered, illustrate its figures and its message so well that I hope all students of the Temple of the Stars will read it, and not depend on this all-too-brief survey. It has recently been re-published by Rilco from an old copy. Morien, Welsh-speaking and an avid researcher into the roots of his ancient tongue, also read Latin, Greek and Hebrew, and was conversant with Egyptian, Jewish and Babylonian mythology; so he was in a better position than most to compare these with that of his Druidic ancestors.

He concludes not only that all these early cultures had a common faith based on observance of the heavenly bodies, but that the similarity of many deities' names shows long intercommunication between east and west. He also shows how much of Christianity was dependent on and stemmed from this earlier universal religion, the essential similarity of both accounting for the relatively peaceful acceptance of the new Faith in Druidic Britain. However, I can only summarise briefly here his findings on the subject of this chapter – the Mabon.

He tells how in Druidic ages the old sun was put in effigy in a coracle or boat at year's end and pushed out over various lakes and rivers in Wales – and in the rest of Britain too before the Romans came. After an absence of forty hours a new effigy, the Mabon or Babe Sun of the new year, was ferried back amid rejoicings. He cites Lakes Llangors and Bala as two such places, and the river Taff at Pontyprydd. But seas were also crossed; the Mediterranean between Phoenicia and the Nile Delta, and the Irish sea between Borth in Cardigan and Arkle in Ireland are given as examples, with Adonis as the Phoenician reborn sun, (also called Iesu-munu, significantly enough), and with the Mabon, Taliesin, Merddyn etc., as his Druidic counterpart in the British Isles.

Morien adds Arthur's name to this list, but it seems that Arthur could be at different times both the old and new sun, for elsewhere he is cited as the dying sun of the Druidic festival of Alban Arthan, the winter solstice. The Glastonbury Zodiac supports both roles, for Arthur-Sagittarius' month ends with the winter solstice, while the young Arthur draws his sword from the lake in a boat, like Gemini.

In other words, he draws his manhood from the sea-mother, and at death must return it whence it came. This verse from the 6th century is illuminating.

"The Crowned Baby Boy, so says Bardism
Will strengthen Britain from the rising sea,
When a fleet will come to Caer Ceri (Barry, Glamorgan)
Then woe to the Saxons with their rabble."
                                                    Iolo MSS.

Another in the same vein suggests a similar ceremony on land, involving a cave, fogou or perhaps a dolmen or a passage-grave.

"The Crowned Babe shall pass through a long tunnel,
Woe to the chief of the tents."

Both quotations express Bardic hopes of deliverance from their enemies through their belief in the potent revival of their sun-god. Alas, they were doomed to disappointment. But the ways of Providence are at the time inscrutable, and when we with hindsight see the stabilising effect of Saxon genes on our volatile Celtic heritage, we may even admit that perhaps it was all for the best? But I digress.

The young sun in his mother's lunar womb-boat was mere inert matter, says Morien, until fertilised by three bars of light from her sky-consort Celu, the Hidden God. God breathed His name IA (Jah) and there was Light. These letters the Druids put together to form the Broad Arrow V (their A was written upside-down like V) -- a mark still used today on trig-points and Government property. It was printed all over convicts' uniforms until recently; a fascinating piece of symbolism, though doubtless unconscious.

This Broad Arrow was depicted all over the ancient world as a descending dove; the Druids also saw it as a wren, the smallest of birds, whose nest is a globe in shape, so that it completely conceals its occupant. Its global shape suggested to them the world, or even a human head, into which the spirit invisibly descended. This IA became IAO, God inspiring the world. (Similar thinking produced such names as Jove, Io, Iona, Jehovah, John.) Druids called the Arrow-Bird White-wings, or Awen.

The wren derived its name, however, from Urien, the British form of Greek Ouranos the sky-god, father of Kronos. But Urien is cited in Celtic legend as the father of the Mabon; thus our Youth is semi-divine, exactly as depicted in the Glastonbury Zodiac in his mother's lunar or crescent boat, with the dove (or wren) hovering above.

Hesiod in the 9th century BC tells how Ouranos or Uranus loved Gaia the earth, and descending to her fathered the twelve Titans; huge giants, who after a furious war with the gods were banished to the far west, "where among impenetrable shadows and foul vapours at the very end of the world, by the will of the king of the heavens, they are buried."

This awful place can only be on the northern shores of the Atlantic. It is difficult to avoid the conclusion that Cretan and Phoenician merchant-mariners had told Hesiod of the Glastonbury Giants - or that the Mabon, one of Ouranos' sons, was among them. (We can only agree, reluctantly, with Hesiod's view of our climate.)

Druidic Mysteries also pictured the Three Bars of Light as three drops of oil (Christos in Greek) which flew out of Ceridwen's Cauldron onto Little Gwion's finger as he stirred it; scalded, he popped it in his mouth and became at once inspired. But all unwitting, he had swallowed the essence of the brew she had been preparing for a year according to the recipe of the Mysteries of the Pheryllt, a Druidic order of alchemists, which she designed for her ugly son Avagddu (Black-Wings) - in the hope that he, though no beauty, might at least have brains. Gwion, now omniscient, knew that she would destroy him if she could, and fled, using his new-found magical powers, in the form of a hare. But she pursued as a greyhound, so he became a fish; she an otter; so he became a bird, but she overtook him as a hawk until he in desperation became a grain of wheat, one of millions on a threshing-floor. But Ceridwen then became a black-crested hen, found him and swallowed him. And that, she thought, was that. But no; nine months later she bore him, a babe so much more beautiful than her ugly son she hadn't the heart to strangle him; so instead she put him in a leather bag (some versions say a coracle) and threw him out to sea to take his chance on the waves.

He drifted to the weir of Gwyddno Garanhir, where Gwyddno's unlucky son Elphin had been put to a fishing test on May-day. If he could not catch a fish then, when the weir was rippling with salmon, then he would be judged unfit to succeed his father. But all Elphin caught was Gwion in his leather bag. The compassionate prince, however, took him home amid the jeers of the courtiers – and was startled and not a little comforted by the babe, who addressed a long oracular poem to him from the saddle-bag.

Gwion was reborn as Taliesin Radiant-Brow! Elphin fostered the child-prodigy, and before long his court became famous for inspired bardism.

When Elphin was imprisoned by King Maelgwyn of North Wales, Taliesin freed him by proposing a riddling test with Maelgwyn's bards which they were unable to solve, and by magic reduced them to blubbering "Blerwm, Blerwm", fingers on lips, as children do.

It is clear that we are among the Druidic Mysteries in this tale, which lady Charlotte Guest included in her translation of the Mabinogion. Prince Elphin, imprisoned like the Mabon and only rescued by superior bardic wisdom, the deaths and rebirths of the infant sun-king, the bubbling Cauldron of Inspiration and Rebirth, all proclaim it. Taliesin's shape-shifting flight from the old Nature-Goddess conceals I believe (though the order is jumbled, perhaps deliberately, or by re-telling) the Druid doctrine of the spirit's evolution from the simplest through ever more complex life-forms until it culminates in Man. Nor is mere animal-man as we are now, the end of the process. Taliesun, as Morien spells his name, is not only the Tall or Raised-up sun, but Tal-Iesin, Jesu – the Essence – Man raised by ever-heightening consciousness to Godhead.

The Three Heavenly Drops reappear in Grail legend as drops of Holy Blood that drip from the point of the Lance in the Grail Procession. They are caught in a vessel borne by a maiden; a variation on the theme of the Cauldron or Lunar boat. When Gawain, all unprepared for these Mysteries, visits Grail Castle, three drops of blood fall on the table where he sits, watching the Procession. He is dumbfounded, and can neither move nor speak, being rendered incapable of asking the vital Grail Question which alone can restore the Maimed king to health, and is ushered from the castle in disgrace. (Perlesvaus Branch 6 Title 19).

The pawnbroker's Three Golden Balls also derive ultimately from this same sign - though more immediately from the three bags of gold that St Nicholas threw into the bedroom of three girls to save them from a life of prostitution to which their bankrupt father was about to consign them as he had no dowry to procure them husbands.

But St Nicholas (shortened to Santa Claus, the Christmas benefactor of the young), was originally Nicor, goat-god of the winter solstice, or Capricorn. Father Christmas' reindeer wear Capricorn horns. Nicor was worshipped at fords in pre-Christian times in deference to the immersion of the winter solstitial sun in water before its self-renewal. St Nicholas also resuscitated three little boys who had been salted down in a tub by some Sweeny Todd or other to make pork pies. This image too was doubtless derived from pagan ones of the babe sun rising from his boat, cauldron or barrel; three babes instead of one perhaps in memory of the Three reviving Drops or three-pronged Awen. These are signed in our Zodiac not only by the Dove but also by three sacred points in the circle's centre, as Katharine Maltwood shows in her "Temple of the Stars".

Morien tells us that the Mabon too was called "Son of the Boat", and that the drawing of this babe from the water was annually celebrated in many places in Wales as the popular festival of Mab Sant, only being suppressed in the early years of the 19th century. Doubtless Wesleyan reformers regarded its "pagan" origins with a jaundiced eye. However one can see how such an ancient festival gave rise to so many "St Mabons" in the early Celtic church.

I will end this survey with an ancient fragment from the Welsh Archaeology quoted in translation by Lewis Spence in his "Mysteries of Britain". It shows the Mabon not only as son of the Creator but also as one of the guardians of these Mysteries.

"Arthur: What man is he that guards the gate?
Hierophant: The severe hoary one with the wide dominion – who is he that demands it?
Arthur: Arthur and the Blessed Kai.

Hierophant: What good attends thee, thou blessed one, thou best man in the world? Into my house thou canst not enter unless thou wilt preserve.

Kai: I will preserve it and that thou shalt behold; though the birds of wrath should go forth and the three attendant ministers should fall asleep, namely the son of the Creator, Mabon, attendant upon the wonderful supreme Ruler, and Gwyn, the Lord of those who descend from above.

Hierophant: Severe have my servants been in preserving their institutes. Manawyddan, the son of Llyr, was grave in his counsel, Manawyd truly brought a perforated shield from Trevryd; and Mabon the son of Lightning, stained the straw with clotted gore: and Anwas the winged and Llwch Llawinog (the ruler of the lakes) were firm guardians of the encircled mount. Their Lord preserved them and I rendered them complete. Kay! I solemnly announce though all three should be slain, when the privilege of the grove is violated, danger shall be found."

Impossible that these heavenly guardians should be found sleeping at their posts! It is tempting to see this bare possibility as a reference to Gemini, whose drooping head has often caused his personifications to be portrayed that way. Did not the speaker, Kai, himself, behead Arthur's Geminian son Lohot in his sleep? That Kai is here called the Blessed confirms this extract as an early one, for here he is on a level with Arthur, "best of men", and worthy to be a candidate for guardianship of the Druidic Mysteries. It is clear that he suffered the fate of most old gods, becoming a devil in the new dispensation. He may in earlier times have been the successor to the dying sun of winter, as his murder of Lohot, son of the old sun Arthur, may indicate. My perhaps naive interpretation of Kai as Caelum – sky – seems justified by his high status in this old Celtic fragment.

Mabon son of Mellt – Lightning – may confuse those who know him as the son of Urien, or Uranus. Has the Mabon two fathers? Or are there two Mabons? No. Uranus holds the lightning-streak in his hand, and we recall the birth-storm of St David, when lightning split the rock where David's mother St Nunn gave him birth. This lightning is, of course, the Logos, Awen or descending Dove from heaven, making David, like the Mabon, half-divine. The two fathers of the Mabon are one; or rather, one is the divine extension of the other.

The Mabon's clotted blood staining the straw must refer to his imprisonment in the Castle of Bones, flesh, or human folly, the prison of Oeth and Anoeth at Caer Loyw or Logres. Were the Lloegrians, whose kingdom we have seen reason to identify with the Glastonbury Zodiac, the people of the Logos, the Word?

Two saints, Elphin and Gwyddno, appear in the Iolo MSS; Elphin as a monk of the monastery of Llantwit; but Baring-Gould dismisses them, not surprisingly, as the characters of the Taliesin story in Christian guise.

CHAPTER 6

ST MATERNUS of Madrun, near Penzance, must once have been Modron, the great Earth-Mother of the Mabon; the name Madrun betrays her. But she has long been subjected to a sex-change. Her well was famous for healing cripples; no doubt she had a special compassion for them, as the dying god, her son, was the Maimed Grail-king of Avalon.

ST MADRON is doubtless another alias of his mother, though said to be a daughter of Vortimer. She and her maid, St Annun or Anhun, both had an identical dream at the same time, as they slept under a bush on their pilgrimage to Bardsey, telling them to found a church at Transfynydd in Merioneth, which they duly obeyed. But is Annun not Ceridwen's Cauldron of Annwn, baptised? (Prophetic? Transfynydd is now a nuclear power station. Annwn indeed! The underworld: ruled by Pluto, or Plutonium).

St GENGULF or WINWALOE, son of Fracan, was cousin to Arthurian Duke Cador of Cornwall; his mother was daughter to Breton King Emir Llydaw. They emigrated to Brittany c 460. He is patron-saint of Anneot, near Avallon in France. He appears first as youthful guard to Pepin the Short, (anachronistically!) and not an efficient one, for he falls asleep on duty in his master's tent. Pepin noticed a light burning above Gengulf's head, and rose from sleep to put it out. But the lamp magically relit itself. This happened three times, and instead of irritably cutting Gengulf's sleepy head off, as might be expected, Pepin was impressed and took it as a sign of his young guard's sanctity. (Winwaloe, his Cornish name, means "bright, shining or holy Gael". He is remembered at Gunwalloe near Mullion, the Initial W of his name already becoming G on his way to France.)

Pepin advanced him to the castle of Avallon, and Gengulf married. But his wife was unfaithful to him, and with Christlike compassion, he let her go with her lover – even endowing them generously with lands – and lived alone, a sad dejected figure. But the greedy pair wanted more, and his wife's lover stealing into the castle at night, seized the sword that hung over Gengulf's bed to kill him as he slept. Gengulf, however, awoke and threw up his arm to ward off the blow, so that it wounded him fatally in the thigh instead. The assassin escaped, and Gengulf died soon after. His body was brought to Varennes by two of his aunts amid great scenes of public anguish; the guilty pair were caught, and Baring-Gould tells us he can't bring himself to describe the horrors of their punishment, even in Latin.

This tragic legend reads like the pre-Christian scenes of public mourning for the dying, young and ever-benevolent sun-and-seed-god, but several factors hint he was connected specifically with the Gemini figure of Avalon, and that his figure and form was known to the teller of the tale. As we have seen, Gemini is often depicted sleeping or sad in Celtic myth, from his lolling head. Gengulf is caught napping twice, and his castle of Avallon can hardly be unconnected with Avalon; the thrice-lit lamp may describe the three Bars of Light above Gemini, making him indeed bright, shining, holy Winwhal. The Geminian upraised arm recurs; the fatal groin wound is endemic to sun-myth, making him Avallach the Maimed Grail-King of Avalon; so are the faithless wife and lover, and the mourning queens, here acted by Gengulf's two aunts. Cornish Winwaloe's mother Gwen had three breasts to feed her three boys; biologically unlikely but mythically quite in order if she was the Earth-Mother with many hungry mouths to feed. Lastly, Gengulf's death was mourned on May 11th near the period of Gemini.

Significantly, his twin brothers SS Jacut and Gwethenoc are also identified with the Zodiacal Twins, for sailors invoked their aid in storms. They would appear (like Castor and Pollux of Jason's Argo), one at the bows, one at the stern, and steer the vessel safely into port. They gave early signs of sanctity, for while yet boys, pupils of St Budoc, they gave sight to the blind and healed a leper. Gwethenoc is patron of St Enodoc, Cornwall.

LITTLE ST HUGH. The later St Hugh of French Avallon, who was brought over by Henry II to be Abbot of Witham Priory in Somerset and then made Bishop of Lincoln, had the name of Hu the sun-god; a coincidence which, taken with the cult of St Gengulph in the same place, seems to indicate that the French town was, like the British Avalon, an ancient Celtic ritual centre. The identical names can hardly be accidental.

Lincoln, by another curious coincidence, remembers two St Hughs; the other, "Little Sir Hugh", was a murdered boy, scourged and crucified by the Jews, or so Matthew Paris records. In mediaeval days, Jews were liable to be blamed for such deaths; it was profitable, for when condemned their property was forfeit to the Church. The cult of the little "saint" was equally profitable, bringing many pilgrims to his shrine. Mathew Paris' account was designed to equate the little victim with Jesus' sufferings at his Passion – but Jesus did not die in infancy, so one feels that the horror and pity that this murder aroused evoked more archetypal wailing for the young and dying sun-and-seed-god. That this may be so is hinted in

Chaucer's Prioress' Tale, where the murdered innocent is visited by the Virgin, to whom in life he had a great devotion. She puts a grain of corn on his tongue (Virgo of the wheatsheaf, surely) which miraculously allows him to sing in her honour although his throat is cut, until his sorrowing parents led by the sound discover his body and exact vengeance on the murderers.

This pre-Christian theme was universally popular up and down the country, to judge by the widely separated areas where these dirges are still sung. It is significant that the little victim is always a boy; for little girls get murdered too, but do not seem to inspire dirges in the same way – yet another reason for suspecting ancient sun-myth underlies their survival. In the two examples here given, both little victims bear sun-god names. Here is a Scottish version:

"Mother, Mother, make my bed, Make for me a winding-sheet,
Wrap me up in your cloak of gold; See if I can sleep."
Four-and-twenty bonny boys, Playing at their ball
Along came Little Sir Hugh Where no-one dared to go.
Out there came a lady gay She was dressed in green
"Come in, come in, Little Sir Hugh And fetch your ball again."
"I can't come in, I won't come in Without my playmates all
For if I should I know you would Cause my blood to flow."
She took him by the milk-white hand And led him to the hall
Till they came to a stone chamber Where none could hear him call.
She sat him in a golden chair She gave him sugar sweet
She laid him on a dressing board And stabbed him like a sheep.
Out there came the thick thick blood And out there came the thin
Out there came the bonny heart's blood Till none was left within.
She took him by the yellow hair And all so fine and neat
She threw him in the old stone well Fifty fathoms deep.
"Mother, Mother, make my bed Make for me a winding-sheet
Wrap me up in your cloak of gold See if I can sleep."

Poor little Sir Hugh; his ball, his yellow hair and the twenty-four playmates all hint at solar origins. Doubtless as these are two too many for a football game they stand for the hours of the day. And the Lady of the Castle? Dressed in green, is she not the Earth-goddess, who bears all her sons away?

In the second sample, Anti-Semitism again rears its ugly head; it comes from Somerset. There *should* be a dirge surviving in the Summer county of Gemini's dying babe.

Easter Day was a holiday of all days in the year
And all the little schoolfellows went out to play, but Sir William was
not there.
Mama went to the Jew's wife's house and knocked at the ring
Saying "Little Sir William, if you are there, pray let your mother in."
The Jew's wife came to the door and said "He is not here today,
He's with the little schoolfellows out on the green, playing some pretty
play."
Mama went to the Boyne water that is so wide and deep
Saying "Little Sir William if you are there, pray pity your mother's
weep."
"How can I pity your weep Mother, and I so long in pain?
For the little penknife sticks close to my heart, and the Jew's wife hath
me slain.
Go home, go home, my mother dear, and prepare my winding-sheet
For tomorrow morning before eight of the clock, you with my body
shall meet.
And lay my prayerbook at my head, and my grammar at my feet
That all the little schoolfellows passing by, may read as they me greet."

This emphasis on reading and using the mind is characteristic of the
Celtic church - not of the Roman. The Christlike analogy is also implied,
as with Matthew Paris. Little Sir William was already dead by Easter Day,
and promised to appear to his mother, as to Mary Magdalen. But the sun
at this season also rose before eight of the clock - and Christ was not
drowned with a penknife in his heart. The name William is compounded
of Hu and Wylo, to weep; the Welsh royal name Hwyll or Howell is a sun-
title. The penknife too is intriguing, for a pen was always a quill. And was
the Boyne water a relic of the sacred river of Ireland, inserted by Irish
monks, of which there were many at Glastonbury in St Patrick's time? Or
was it simply the Boy's water?

The Welsh name Pwyll (Powell to you and me) means a pool, originally
Ap-Hwyl, or the son of the sun, who was understood to have been
reflected, or drowned, in water. There is a hidden wealth of Celtic myth
in these short syllables; for them, every willow by every pool or stream is
weeping for the dying young god. Celts understood the Incarnation before
Christianity, and by means of such songs, the Celtic church strove to adapt
the old Faith to the New.

ST RIOCHE. This Breton saint's legend is more entertaining than credible, and seems to exhale memories of our Zodiac's Gemini babe, carried to Brittany.

When he was only two, his father Elwrn, a landowner of Landernac, threw himself into the river at Brezal in despair, but was rescued by two travellers, Neventer and Derrian, returning from the Holy Land. This we are told was at the time when Helena was searching there for the True Cross, that is, about 325 AD.

Enquiring the cause of Elwrn's desperate act, they were told that a fierce dragon was ravaging Brittany, and king Bristoc of Brest had resorted to casting lots among his subjects to find its next meal. So many of Elwrn's retainers had been devoured that he only had his wife and young son left when the lot once again fell upon him to provide the next victim, and rather than sacrifice them he had decided to drown himself.

Neventer and Derrian were made of sterner stuff, and promised to rid the country of the monster if Elwrn would commit his young son to a Christian ascetic life when of age. Elwrn consented, and the two heroes went to find the dragon. Tracing it to its lair, Derrian fearlessly threw his baldric over its neck. This tamed it at once, and the 2-year old child – the future St Rioche – led it unresisting to his father's castle, from whence it was thrown into the sea.

Rioche, true to his promised vocation, retired at the tender age of fifteen to a rocky islet in the parish of Camaret and lived in hermetic solitude for 44 years. He was eventually found by Fragan, a British emigrant, completely overgrown with red moss! Undismayed, Fragan scraped him clean and finding healthy white flesh beneath, gave him to his son St Winwaloe who took him to Landewenec to be cared for until he died, around 530.

530? But we are told he was born about 325. Over 200 years is a long life even for a fossilised hermit. Easier to believe that St Rioche was a sacred rock or stone, as his name and mossiness hints - baptised into Christianity perhaps by Fragan and Winwaloe. But this explanation does not account for the legend that this hoary hermit-stone was once a two-year old child who led a defeated dragon home in triumph.

Fragan and his son Winwaloe were of royal Cornish blood; Fragan was cousin to duke Cado of Cornwall in Arthurian times, and probably fled to Brittany to escape a quarrel of succession; as scions of a royal House they must have inherited the Zodiac Secret. Winwaloe is patron of several Cornish churches - not least Landewednack on the Lizard. It seems he named Brittany's Landewenec (Rioche's sanctuary) after his home-town in Britain. There are many such place-names in Brittany, transferred by homesick British migrants.

Celtic Christianity contained many Druidic elements. Did the missionary Winwaloe also transfer Gemini's hill-figure to the rocky islet of Camaret, to illustrate by Gemini the triumph of light over darkness, good over evil – mediating thus between the old Nature-worship and the new Christianity? Was Camaret Breton for Camelot?

And did the dragon stand for the Zodiac's Whale, or the circumpolar constellation of Draco? The Whale or Leviathon swallows the dying sun-king, as the sea swallows the setting sun; but Draco at the Zenith of the night sky symbolises the temporary ascendence of the powers of darkness. Both are overcome by Rioche's young sun.

We have seen this dragon tamed before, in the Lives of both Petroc and Carantoc, two saints whose fantastic adventures seem inexplicable until decoded by the Zodiac; and the legend of Winwaloe himself shows him in the Geminian guise of the benevolent and dying young sun-king.

These saints, and others like St Melor, suggest that British missionaries of this period blended compatible elements of the older religion into their Christian evangelisation on the Continent; indeed, they would be welcomed and recognised, for Druidic influence still lingered in many rural parts of France away from the Romanised centres. Winwaloe's French Avallon is an intriguing pointer; another is the mediaeval belief that Arthur's Round Table was brought to England from Brittany in 1087 by Rhys ap Tudor. What he brought back was not a piece of antique furniture, surely – but knowledge of the Zodiac, lost to Britain during the centuries of Saxon and Danish invasion.

ST ROCH of Roche and Rock near Padstow, both in Cornwall, may simply be a hermit who lived under the rock – but in view of the above legend, he may be yet another mossy memorial of Gemini on his hill.

Two shadowy characters occur in Malory's lists of Arthurian knights, Sir Melot de la Roche and Sir Melion of the Mountain. As only their names remain, their exploits long forgotten, this suggests that they are ancient and fading sun-gods in series with Sir Meliot of Logres and little St Melor. It will be recalled that the holy child Melor, a Celtic sun-god by virtue of his silver hand, lay down on top of a mountain (like Gemini) and thus became invisible to his murderous pursuers. We first meet Sir Meliot of Logres in the High History as a fearless child of six who rides round an orchard on a lion; surely Gemini and Leo in Avalon's orchard? Seeing Gawain, the child kneels to him in homage, raising his joined hands to him. A more accurate picture of young Gemini could hardly be drawn. Later on when a grown man he encounters and kills the Knight of the Galley, "that sings in the sea." But this must have been one of his own titles, for Gemini kneels in the Cancerian Galley. He also kills the knight's dwarf – which can be another reference to Gemini. In his next adventure Meliot rescues his hero Gawain from the Lion. There seems little doubt where we are on the Zodiac.

Melor and Meliot both die young; both are killed by treachery, typical of young sun-kings.

King Meliagrance of Melwas is another similarly-named Arthurian character connected with that most prominent of hills — the Tor — and he too plays the sun-king's role by stealing earthy Guinevere from Arthur; being forced to return her when the seasons change.

There is also an enigmatic knight in Malory's tale of Balin and Balan, who passes Arthur "making great dole." When Arthur asks him the cause of his grief, he merely replies "Ye may little amend me" and goes on his way to the Castle of Meliot. We never learn the reason for his sorrow, for he, like Melor and Meliot, is soon killed by treachery, this time by the invisible evil knight Garlon, the very spirit of darkness. Here again, I believe, Gemini the Man of Sorrows, has passed by.

Melias de l'Isle, Galahad's young squire, is another of the same ilk, a sort of shadow of his hero, for Galahad is surely Gemini par excellence. And though Melias is described as a prince of Denmark, that country is hardly an island. It seems more likely that like Meliot of Logres, his isle was originally the Isle of Avalon, on whose hill reposes the primordial Bowed One of the Mound.

At the end of Chapter 1, I have given reasons for believing that all these Meliot-related names go way back through the ages to the Phoenician word Melek (king) and to their Trinity, from which several Welsh royal houses derive their ancestry, and from whom comes Avallach, the Maimed king of Avalon.

St ROCHE OF MONTPELLIER. If Geminian legends have penetrated deep into France to adhere to Gengulph-Winwaloe and Rioche, then we may also suspect Montpellier's St Roche, whom Baring-Gould dismisses as entirely legendary. Nor does Butler deign to mention him in his otherwise encyclopoedic list of saints. The lack of verifiable facts about him is odd, for his tale dates him to the 14th century, when there were plenty of monastic scribes around to record his history. But despite this credibility-gap, he became enormously popular; it is as though he represented the ideal man of primitive Christianity, an ideal lost sight of by popes and princely cardinals of the time. With extreme cruelty and mass-murder, they had recently exterminated the Cathar "heresy" in the south of France, laying waste its cities and countryside. Montpellier was a Cathar centre in the 12th – 13th century; its surviving citizens badly needed someone to believe in, and a focus for expressing their horror of man's cruelty to man.

The Templars too had recently been suppressed by the Inquisition with equal cruelty; both Cathars and Templars regarded themselves as Guardians of the Grail. And where the Grail was held in veneration, the Christlike figure of Gemini could not be far away — in fact in more than one exposition of the sacred Vessel, he appears, rising from it as a Babe who becomes a crucified man — a convincing portrayal of his dual effigy in the Glastonbury Vessel.

St Francis of Assissi was the outstanding reformer of Church values at this period. As his mother was a native of Provence it must be wondered how much he learnt from her about the Cathar "perfecti", those barefoot teachers and healers whose exemplary lives made such a glaring contrast to the Catholic priesthood, high and low. But although he was reluctantly allowed to found his mendicant Franciscan order within the Church, its worldly princes viewing him with scornful wonder give no sign of changing their ways. So the huge popularity of St Roche's legend about a century after Francis' death seems to show a continuing need for protest.

Roche like Francis was high-born and wealthy, but left his wealth with an uncle to go on pilgrimage to Rome. But he was overwhelmed on his way by the sufferings of the people of Aquapendente, who were stricken by the plague. He stayed to help them and is said to have healed thousands, but at last succumbed to the plague himself.

Lying sick and near to death, he was found by a dog who became his faithful companion, stealing food wherever he could to keep his adopted master alive. Eventually he revived, and wandered plague-scarred and tattered back to his home-town of Montpellier, where his uncle was a magistrate. But this uncle didn't, or wouldn't, recognise him, and had him thrown in prison as a spy. (Though Baring-Gould's account doesn't identify the magistrate with the uncle who kept Roche's wealth, if they were indeed one and the same it gives good reason for his failure to recognise and reinstate his nephew).

Here he remained, hungry and neglected for five years until he died. But when they found his emaciated body, his cell was flooded with unearthly light.

Another legend, at variance with the one above, insists that he not only reached Rome, but had the temerity to make the sign of the cross with his finger on the brow of a cardinal, leaving a mark that defied all attempts to erase it. Christlike, Roche was thus judging Rome and finding it wanting.

Was he not simply an image of Christ, set up to shame the Church of his day? Why drag in Grail or Celtic elements to account for him? But Christ had no wicked uncle, no dog, did not languish long in prison, and was not smitten in the thigh - though his side, pierced on the cross, may well be a euphemism for the sun-king's traditional wounding. (St Roche, with his dog beside him, is often represented lifting his robe to show the plague-spot on his thigh; he can be seen thus in a mediaeval panel in Romsey Abbey.) But these are all characteristics of Gemini with his Great Dog - or of Celtic saints or heroes that derive from him.

It is not only his reverberating name that has allowed St Roche to find a place in this collection. Though manifestly not Celtic himself, there are certainly reasons for seeing him as Celt-inspired; not least among them the doubt about his existence. He hovers in true Celtic style between reality and the super-real. Nor need we doubt whether these legends could have penetrated so far south as Italy; Celtic saints were there long before him, and Arthur and his knights appear sculptured on Modena Cathedral and elsewhere in the early 1100's. In truth, in the ensuing century legends of Arthur and the mystic Grail swept across all Europe like a Pentecostal wind; as one Alanus wrote, "Whither has not the flying fame spread and familiarised the name of Arthur the Briton, even as far as the empire of Christendom extends? Who does not speak of Arthur the Briton, since he is almost better known to the peoples of Asia Minor than to the Britanni?"

ST WILLOW of Lanteglos near Fowey in Cornwall was another decapitated hermit whose chief claim to fame was that after he was killed he walked from St Willow's bridge to the church with his head under his arm. He was originally St Gwodloew, patron of Lantegros near Fowey, and grandson of the brigand-turned Saint Gwynllyw of Monmouth. His killer was a near kinsman called Mellin — a name whose variations call up a host of solar associations, as we have seen. And as Willow was killed near a bridge (at Pont Polruan), it is reasonable to suspect that this was a place long remembered for the ritual duel between sun-kings who fought by the water's edge; its victim being sanctified, to ensure a smooth transition to Christianity. The name Willow, too, evokes Little Sir William, and reminds one of the tree of the high god Esus.

Morien Morgan however has another derivation for Wil- words, pointing out that Gwylle was the Druidic name for another solar ritual, where the old sun was put in effigy in a boat to pass through the river of death. This river, from which the young renewed sun emerged reborn, was known to the Druids as Gwyllionwy. He instances the town of Wilton near Salisbury with its river Wylye as one such place, and shows the Arms of the Abbey as evidence; pictured within a vesica piscis is a chapel, in whose crypt is immured a human figure, while above the roof a new born babe flies upward. The church, he says, thus transmuted the Druid tradition into its own, for its nave (navis) is the boat in Christian guise. The abbey was dedicated to St Denis - another decapitated saint who walked with his head in his hands, like St Willow. If Morien is right in asserting that Wilton was a Druid Mystery site, the substitution of St Denis for the original god was apt; for Denis of France was once Dionysus, paramount in the Orphic Mysteries, who harrowed Hades to free his mother Semele and translate her to Olympus. He was another god who was killed and resurrected, triumphant over death. Note the Ysus in his name.

Another wide-spread version of the sun's rebirth is that he was born in a cave at the winter solstice. So it is interesting to find St Willow's cave near this bridge. It is still pointed out as his hermitage. Let us assume that a Celtic Christian hermit was placed there, to baptise the ancient sacred site, and that some of its memories were transferred to him.

ST HUAIL is yet another battling sun-god, as his legends, and his name (from haul the sun) imply. Caradoc of Llancarfan's Life of Gildas tells how he had the temerity to court the same lady as Arthur. The two rivals fought until Huail wounded Arthur in the thigh – upon which Arthur called off the fight on condition that Huail should never refer to his humiliation on pain of death. But Arthur always limped after that.

Shortly afterwards Arthur fell for another lady at Ruthin, and danced with her, clad unaccountably in female attire... Huail watching them, couldn't resist a jibe, and said "his dancing might do very well but for the thigh." Arthur overheard him break their bargain and in fury ordered Huail to be taken out and forthwith beheaded in Ruthin's St Peter's Square on a stone called to this day Maen Huail.

Huail was Gildas' brother, and Gerald of Wales says that this family feud was the reason why Gildas never mentioned Arthur's name in his book. Arthur we are told had to pay Gildas blood-money for this beheading. There were other incidents in this feud, for Huail according to the Mabinogion had previously stabbed Arthur's nephew Gwydre, "and hatred was between Huail and Arthur because of the wound." If Huail was a historical character he seems to have been a free–booting tearaway, always in a fight; as a son of King Caw of Strathclyde, expelled from the family lands by Picts, he perhaps had a perpetual chip on his shoulder. Caw and his clan were given refuge by Maelgwyn of North Wales; for Gildas to have castigated Maelgwyn, his family's protector, so venomously in his Complaining book argues a degree of ingratitude which is astonishing.

Caradoc reports that "Huail submitted to no king, not even Arthur." and Baring-Gould comments that he richly deserved beheading, by all accounts.

Hast thou heard the saying of Huail
Son of Caw the cautious reasoner?
"Often will a curse drop out of the bosom."
Sayings of the Wise

He was like that! Not much of a saint. In fact it could be argued that his sainthood was conferred not because of his character, but because of the sun-myth that became attached to him by his name. The wound in the thigh is of course a recurring theme; Robert Graves' White Goddess has some interesting remarks on the lame sun-hero, noting too that even Achilles, Hercules and Dionysus all spent periods confined to women's quarters, dressed in female attire and spinning. This he puts down to the sun-hero's infancy; a philosophical reminder that even the greatest are dependent on women at the outset of their glorious careers. Jungians doubtless have more to say here on the hidden anima in the male.

The thigh in myth always has godlike attributes - it is even a godlike word, being Theo in old English, Deo in old German. Doubtless a euphemism for castration, this wound makes Arthur the Maimed King of Avalon, his rival Huail playing the part of Scorpionic Mordred, ruled by Mars, and his martial quality is emphasised in the Triads, where he appears as "One of the Three Diademed Battle Chiefs of the Isle of Britain."

Nonetheless, Huail has his statue at Melrand in Brittany, the villagers still processing to it up to the early 1900s to pray for rain in times of drought. Perhaps they still do? Did Huail become a rain-god – despite his sun name – because he always opposed Arthur the sun?

ST HYWEL, yet another in this series of sun-names, son of Emir Llydaw of Brittany, became one of Arthur's knights - a common fate for forgotten sun-gods. One of the Three Royal Knights in the triads, invincible, yet "so amiable in manner and gentle in speech that no-one could refuse them anything they asked." A very different character from Huail.

ST KENELM of Clent in Worcestershire, (10 miles south west of Birmingham) is another doubtful little martyr. Though in legend he succeeds his father Cenwulf, king of Mercia, in 819 and is murdered shortly afterwards by his ambitious sister Quendrida, the Anglo-Saxon Chronicle knows nothing of him or his killing, and simply states that Cenwulf was succeeded by Ceolwulf. The legend however was popular, appearing in several early accounts, the first we have being Matthew of Westminster's and William of Malmesbury's (1120).

Kenelm's elder sister was jealous of the little boy-king, and conspired with her lover Askobert to seize his throne. Askobert on pretence of

Tympanum, St Kenelm's, Clent

hunting took Kenelm from Winchcombe, then the Mercian capital, to Clent and there cut off his head and buried him under a thorn. A distinctly ritual element creeps into one account, where Kenelm, unafraid, insists that the deed must not be done until he sticks his ash-staff into the ground at the right time and place. Needless to say it puts forth leaves at once. (Odin hung on the World-Ash-Tree Ygdrasil for nine nights; Assher was the sun-god over much of Asia, and doubtless named that continent). A white cow came lowing to the grave and would not move from it. Kenelm's spirit rose as a dove and flew to St Peter's, Rome, where it deposited a scroll before the Pope which read in Anglo-Saxon

"In Clent, in Cowbage, Kenelm king-born
Lyeth under a thorn, his head off-shorn".

Messengers were sent to England, finding the grave by the lowing of the faithful cow, and when the little body was exhumed a spring of healing water welled up, curing many – among them not only one boy whose *calves adhered to his thighs, but* two. (An astonishingly common malformation apparently in earlier days, reminding us of St Keneth, whose name so resembles Kenelm's).

The body of Kenelm was taken to Winchcombe to lie beside his father. As the sad procession approached the abbey bells rang of themselves, and the guilty Quendred ("Dread Queen?") was told that it was because her brother's body was coming home. "She seyd in grete scorne, 'That is as treue as both myne eyen fall upon this booke', and anon both her eyen fell out of her hede upon the booke." She soon died miserably, her guilt plain to all. Serve her right, too. She, I take it, was the dread Earth-Mother who claims us all at death, the white cow being a traditional symbol for her more benevolent aspect. Isis, mourning the dead Osiris, was cowheaded, and Brigit who is suspected of taking on the mantel of Brigantia, is indelibly associated with cows. And what sun-king has not been betrayed by sister, wife or lover?

But these are Anglo-Saxons, not Celts! Nonetheless, Mercia means Welsh Marches-land, and family trees exist which show that their ruling clan the Hwicci or Gewissae were half-British, half-Saxon. (Merlin and Vortigern came from the Land of the Gewissae). The Severn ran through Offa's Mercia, giving easy passage for British myth from Somerset. Seven churches in Gloucestershire, Worcestershire and Herefordshire are dedicated to 7-year-old St Kenelm, and several holy wells, so popular was his cult. The village of Kenelmstowe grew and flourished by it, though since the Reformation and the later diversion of the Bromsgrove-Dudley road it has entirely disappeared, leaving his little church high and solitary on the hills which look down 1000 feet over the Severn valley. Nothing more romantic than its situation can be imagined, nothing more beautiful than its views to Malvern and Shropshire's Clee Hills. Celts fled to such hills when Saxons invaded their more fertile acres; they and their myths survived longer in these fastnesses.

Connections with Somerset are not lacking; Roger de Somery was granted a fair in Kenelmstowe's churchyard by Henry III; Roger de Somerset was its landowner under Edward I. A strange custom persisted until the 19th century of pelting the parson with crab-apples in the churchyard. Were the natives avenging the displacement of Avallach, the Geminian sun-king of Avalon, by the Christian version? Avalon means apple-land.

Near St Kenelm's lies Hagley, which place-name dictionaries say means Haw-ley; but as the hawthorn was the earth-goddess' tree, and as Kenelm was buried beneath a hawthorn, we may suspect that Hagley remembers the goddess in her hag aspect, slayer and devourer of the children she has borne. For all must return their bodies at death to the earth that gave them life. (Was the Christian Crown of Thorns a sharp reminder of Man's mortality?)

Three trees whisper echoes of the Druid Tree-Alphabet on this ancient hill; the ash of the sacrificed god, the thorn of his earth-mother and the apple that exiled man from Eden, and brought death into the world.

I must record yet another astonishing coincidence here. While typing St Kenelm's story, a letter came from Sue Newland, to whom I am indebted for her indefatigable research into this very saint's legend, freely given me. If we were in constant communication this would perhaps not be extraordinary, but as her last notes on St Kenelm came at least six months ago, the timing of this letter is surely remarkable. Is something trying to get through?

ST HELIER c. 540, of the Isle of Jersey is another saint whose sun-name and sad fate makes one suspect that he is one of these doomed young solar gods; especially as the island is strewn with megalithic remains of the ancient sun-cult.

This is his story. A childless Belgian nobleman and his wife were promised a son by a priest, on condition that he should enter the church when of age to do so. In due time Helier was born, and an old monk was charged with his education. A great friendship developed between the two, but Sigebard, Helier's father, unwilling to keep his side of the bargain and ill-pleased to see his son daily growing in piety, attacked the old monk one day and killed him. Appalled, Helier fled (presumably by ship) to a rock off Jersey – the rock on which Elizabeth Castle was later built – and lived there, inflicting himself with every kind of privation. Pirates visited the island, and to escape them the unfortunate boy weakened by these privations could only crawl into a cave to hide, but was betrayed by the screaming of a crowd of seagulls round the cave-mouth and discovered by the pirates, who cut off his head.

The sun, rising full of promise in the east (Belgium contains another form of the solar name) and setting in the far south-west, its strength weakening as it dies?

This suspicion is deepened by a passage culled from "St Patrick's Writing" (translated by Arnold Marsh, 1961), where that saint invokes the sun-name Helia as the sun rises to save him from the temptations of the night. "...Well, on that same night I was sleeping and Satan tempted me powerfully, which will be a memory as long as I am in this body, and he fell on me like a great rock, while nothing in my limbs had any strength. But how did it occur to me in my ignorance to call upon Helias? And meanwhile I saw the sun rise in the sky and while I shouted Helia! Helia! with all my might, lo and behold the splendour of that sun fell down on me and at once smashed off all the weight from me; and I believe I was helped by Christ the Lord ..."

One can only wish that the sea-gulls had been as helpful to poor little St Helier as they were to his Welsh counterpart St Keneth, for in both cases they must symbolise the white-winged Awen of the Druids so often attendant on the Holy Boy – and the Logos descending from the dying sun-king's head to enlighten the world. Incidentally, the word Awen recalls the name St Ouen, patron saint of another of Jersey's maritime parishes.

And is ST CLEMENT, patron saint of yet another seaboard Jersey parish, this same Awen in disguise? Ostensibly, this saint had nothing to do with Jersey – or Cornwall, where he has a parish on the Truro river – being the third Bishop of Rome after St Peter. These were troubled times for the early Church, and a 9th century legend tells how he was arrested in the persecution of the Christians and sentenced to slavery in the marble quarries of Pontus in the Crimea. But as he persisted in converting many pagan convicts there, the prefect ordered him to be taken out to sea and thrown overboard, tied to an anchor to ensure that he drowned. (Earlier accounts say that he died a natural death in the year 102).

But St Clement has become localised in Jersey, where the oldest inhabitants of the parish will still point out his shrine or chapel - one rock among many almost a mile out to sea, and only uncovered at very low tides.

Is St Clement's anchor not the Awen, the Druidic Broad Arrow or White-Wings of the descending Logos, pictured in our Zodiac? Are these two dedications in sailors' parishes in Jersey and Cornwall not a Christian adaptation from more ancient beliefs? Clement means mercy, which descends like the Awen "as the gentle rain from heaven".

An echo of the older gods comes down almost to our own day in one of Frederic Keel's sea-songs -

> "You're young my lad and you're lary
> But if you want to make old bones
> Steer clear of old Mother Carey
> And that there Davey Jones."

By the time this was written down by John Masefield, the sailor-poet, from an old nautical tradition, Mother Carey had become a sea-witch dwelling with her consort Davey Jones down in his locker, crunching drowned sailors' bones. But once they were Virgo the Earth-mother and the descending Logos of Libra; of all "Mother Carey's chickens" – sea-gulls – he must have been her favourite. His name is compounded from Daffydd or Duw Dovydd, God's messenger, and John or Iona, which means much the same; I the Spirit descending into O the world. Saint David, one remembers, had his pet Dove, and Clement's descent into the deep recalls David's birth-storm at sea. Jonah, another "Iona", was also like Clement, heaved into the deep.

The Awen in the form of three silver rods figures in the lives of two other saints, Samson and Brioc. In both cases their mothers are visited by an angel who announces the imminent birth of a son of exceptional spirituality, and commands them to make three silver rods.

Galahad, the Christlike knight, also has three spindles above the bed in which he lies in Solomon's Ship. And though Malory explains them as wooden staves cut from the Tree of Life in Eden, their colours red, white and green, they also suggest the Three Bars of Light, the traditional Druidic mark of inspiration.

Saint, 8th Cent.
Castor Church
Northants

ST KEA COLODOC was, according to Albert Le Grand who wrote his history in 1636, a Cornishman of noble birth who died in 495. Not that Albert knew anything about Cornwall, but the place-names he gives from his more ancient Breton sources are easily traceable to the Truro river, where — no accident surely — is the parish of Old Kea. Here Arthurian memories are strong, especially of King Mark, Tristram and Iseult, and Kea himself has an Arthurian legend, which accounts for his appearance in these pages.

He early became an accomplished scholar and we are told was made a bishop (where is unspecified), giving his ample all to the poor. But deeming himself unworthy of office, he soon resigned and was led by God to St Gildas, apparently a skilled bell-founder, who gave him a bell which as he wandered would ring of itself when he reached a suitable hermitage. At Rosene (Roseland) he caused a fountain to spring up which slaked his companions' thirst and which long after cured the sick. Crossing the arm of the sea called Hildrech (now the Truro river) they entered a forest. There the bell rang. Thanking God, they settled there, helped by local alms and gifts of oxen for ploughing.

But one day a panting stag took refuge in Kea's hut. The saint wouldn't give him up to the hunter, Theodoric of Gudrun Castle (now Goodern), who appears as Teudar, a tyrant, in other saints lives. Enraged, Theodoric made off with Kea's oxen, and when our saint went to ask for them back hit him, striking out a tooth. Kea bore this patiently and went to wash his mouth in a spring — which ever after became famous for curing toothache.

Meanwhile stags from the forest offered themselves to pull the plough - a common miracle in these saintly lives – but this amazing sight only hardened the tyrant's heart. It must have been conscience that shortly afterwards made him so ill; at death's door he sent for Kea, promising him his oxen and much land besides if he would heal him. This our humble saint gladly did, but God was not so easily appeased – and as soon as Theodore recovered and went hunting again, he fell off his horse and broke his neck. Tyrants with Celtic saints on their land take note!

Kea built a monastery on his newly-acquired land, but soon appointed a superior to run it, and left to resume his mendicant life. Resolved on Brittany, he begged a rich merchant for some bread and biscuits to sustain his party on their way, but the merchant mocked him, saying "here is a barge full of corn on the quay; take it, if you can move it." The saint, resigned, set sail, saying only "Blessed be God". But the barge miraculously loosed itself and followed the saints to Brittany; thus providing them with enough corn until they reaped their first harvest at Cleder, where they landed in 472.

This is a miracle unique to St Kea; up till now his miracles have all been drawn from a common saintly stock. It is unkind to suggest that this last, peculiar to him, arose from a pun on Kea and quay?

While Kea was edifying Brittany, King Arthur came campaigning in Gaul, entrusting his wife and kingdom to the treacherous Mordred, who seized Guinevere and allied himself with the invading Saxons. The prelates, alarmed for the Church under this heathen threat, sent Kea to negotiate peace between the King and his nephew-son. But the Saxon army was so huge and bent on destruction that Kea despaired of all negotiation and returned to Brittany, only delaying long enough to persuade Guinevere to take the veil. He died at Cleder, but as his monastery was sacked in later wars his burial-place was forgotten, only being rediscovered by one Britaliensis, who dreamt that if he dug in a certain place, he would find seven bodies, and the one beneath which sprang a welling stream would be Kea's. There would then be an earthquake. All happened as foretold, and a shrine was erected to him at Cleder and other places in both Britains. Eventually, however, monks of Rosene asked for and obtained his relics.

Hagiologists dismiss St Kea's Arthurian adventure, surmising that he has strayed into the legend owing to the similarity of his name to Sir Kay's, Arthur's seneschal. So would I, but for the odd fact that Kea is associated with St Filius or Ffili in several place-names. - and as we have seen, the elusive Ffili was the son of St Keneth and brother of St Eval, all three being identifiable with the Gemini figure.

Canon Doble in his "Saints of Cornwall" has noted that the village of Philleigh (patron saint St Filius in 1311) is opposite that of Kea across the river; that just east of Barnstaple the parish of Landkey (Lan of Kea) is near that of Filleigh; and that in Brittany the parish of St Quay-Portrieux was once known as St Scophili. Authorities think that the two saints once had two chapels near each other, that St (Sco)phili's decayed while Kea's remained and became the parish church. Doble not unreasonably concludes that the two saints were brother-missionaries, working together at these places. It is strange, however, if this is true, that no trace of Fili survives in the Life of Kea. But Kea has another Lan in Somerset, intriguingly near the original "Filius" of Gemini of Dundon Hill. The place-name at Leigh-in-Street has now gone, but appears in a charter of 725 as Lan-to-Kai. Kea, says Canon Doble, was probably a Glastonbury monk who went with others to convert parts of Wales, Devon, Cornwall and Brittany.

Arthurian Sir Kay, too, is connected with Gemini of Dundon Hill just south of Street. An ancient and barbaric tale in the "High History of the

Holy Grail" tells how Lohot, Arthur's son, fought and killed a giant, then – as his strange habit was – lay down on him to sleep. Along comes envious Sir Kay, cuts off Lohot's head and takes it in a casket to Arthur's court, explaining as he shows it that he found Lohot beheaded by the Giant. As he reveals the head, *two* suns shine through opposite windows of the hall at once. What can this tragic tale be but a hoary fragment of sun-myth that has survived into Arthurian legend? But it is even more clearly inspired by Gemini's dual effigy on Dundon and Lollover Hills, where the young son of the old sun-god overlays the Giant Babe, both heads bent at right-angles to the body, suggesting sleep – or decapitation.

It was once an oft-told tale, for a Welsh version also survives in which Kay's victim is Arthur's son Lacheu. (Old Welsh, Lacc=slack, to droop, decline?) In this one Kay attempts to abduct Guinevere (Gwynhwyvar); but this too is essential to the myth, for the earth-goddess must belong alternatively to both summer and winter kings.

It might be thought that Kay is playing here the part of night, in extinguishing the setting sun; but in the Mabinogion's oldest tale "Kulhwch and Olwen" he shows definite traces of solar glory. He can also be a giant.

"Very subtle was Kai. When it pleased him he could render himself as tall as the highest tree in the forest. And he had another peculiarity - so great was the heat of his nature that when it rained hardest, whatever he carried remained dry for a handbreadth above and a handbreadth below his hand; and when his companions were coldest, it was to them as fuel with which to light their fire".

His name suggests a solar deity, if it derives from Caelum, sky. In early Welsh poems he was Arthur's first ally, slaying the great Cath Palug among other lions (Leo?) and hundreds of warriors. Yet in later Arthurian legend, though still his steward and seneschal, he deteriorates into the lying, boastful knight, treacherous to his lord and a bully to dwarves and scullions. A fallen deity indeed. He could hardly be more unlike his namesake St Kea, so humble, patient in adversity, so protective of helpless creatures. Yet both are connected with Arthur's Lohot or Lacheu, or "St Filius", and both appear at the abduction of Guinevere, though one abducts her, the other saves her from it and guides her into chaster ways. Do they not both derive from the earlier sky-god - one to grace (and later disgrace) Arthur's Round Table, the other becoming canonised in Celtic Christian times to wean his adherents into gentler habits of thought and behaviour?

Where to assign Sir Kay the fiery giant, in our Zodiac? For at present he has no seat there, though he should belong to one of the fire-signs. Perhaps his saintly counterpart has given the answer, with his cell at Lan-to-kai -

for it is at Street, on the head of fiery Aries. Yes! For he then would lie next to his father Sir Ector, who in Malory is described as "a man of much property" and must thus be Taurus, – Protector of the Waif Arthur, whom he lovingly oversees in Gemini's Babe. Malory gives a motive for Kay's jealousy of Arthur; for it is not he, but the cuckoo in his nest who draws the sword from the stone, thus proving himself the Chosen King.

ST GERMANUS. The legend of St Keneth sheds startling light on Bede's record of the much-respected Germanus and his anti-Pelagian missions in Britain. Pelagius, a Briton whose real name was Morgan, was our first heretic. Living from about 360 to 420 he must have been a Culdee Christian (a fusion of Druidic and early eastern Christianity.) Uneasy at the growing doctrine of Original Sin, he felt that its effect was to make men lose all self-confidence in their own power of self-improvement and to enslave them too much to church rites as their only hope of salvation. Men had lived good and praiseworthy lives before Christ came, he declared, and he particularly objected to the Church's consigning of unbaptised babes to hell or limbo. At a time when St Augustine of Hippo was teaching predestination, he firmly believed in man's free-will."If I ought, I can", was his favourite dictum.

Heir to a long Druidic tradition of free debate on such important matters, Pelagius was shocked to find himself a "heretic" when he took his ideas to the continent; further shocked too when he reached Rome to find such a low moral tone prevailing there. This must have confirmed his suspicion that if you call people miserable sinners they will soon become so. He must also have felt that such ecclesiastics were hardly fit to hold the keys of salvation so firmly in their hands. Although Pelagius and his following were eventually silenced on the continent by St Augustine in a series of synods, Pelagianism kept raising its heretical head for some years in its homeland, Britain.

St Germanus of Auxerre was twice despatched there to refute it. On his first voyage he was nearly drowned by evil spirits who conjured up a terrible storm. Germanus was asleep when his terrified companions roused him to still the winds and waves, which he did by invoking the Trinity, so that all reached Britain's shore in safety. He quelled the Pelagians more by miraculously healing a blind girl than by preaching, then visited the shrine of St Alban. Returning from this visit, he was snared by the Devil who made him break his leg. The Devil made the country around his hut catch fire, but such was Germanus' sanctity that, helpless as he was, he refused to be moved, trusting in God to save him. And sure enough the flames leapt over his hut leaving him unharmed, and blew themselves out. One would think these miracles would have silenced what Bede calls "this abominable heresy" for ever, but no. A few years later he was again recalled to Britain to quell the Pelagians once more. "Evil spirits" says Bede, were reluctantly compelled to prophesy his coming (clairvoyant Bards, no doubt) so that a chieftain, Elaphius, hurried to meet them hoping that the saint would heal his young crippled son, whose leg was bent and useless. Germanus gently drew the leg "bent with disease" out straight, and healed the lad. This with Germanus' exhortations finally undid the Pelagians, who Bede tells us were banished to the continent to learn from their betters the error of their ways.

But Bede, staunchly Roman in outlook, was writing nearly 300 years after the Pelagian heresy. How much of this account is history, and how much is a distorted memory of the Pelagians' Gemini-boy with the leg bent under him? I ask because it seems curious (to say the least) that Germanus suffered a broken leg himself – and because he is also remembered as sleeping, Gemini-like, in a ship.

If to the Druid-Christian-Pelagians the boy with the crippled leg was their Christ-figure, was the healing of the "crippled boy" the real object of Germanus' mission? In straightening out this leg was the saint seeking to replace this "Christ" with one more orthodox?

St Keneth's incest theme also recurs in the records of Germanus, though the source this time is the "Historia Britonum" of Nennius, written c 800.

Vortigern the British king had rashly invited Hengist the Saxon over to help subdue the invading Picts and Scots, and had fallen deeply in love with Hengist's daughter and married her. Soon after that, Nennius asserts, he married his own daughter and had a son by her. (This seems not only reprehensible but extremely odd, as he was lately so felicitously wedded.) When Germanus heard this he came boldly with all the British clergy to reprove the king. The shameless daughter, prompted by Vortigern, accused Germanus himself of being the father of her child. But Germanus outwitted them by retorting to the child "I will indeed be a Father to you, nor will I dismiss you till a razor, comb and scissors are given to me and it is allowed you to give them to your carnal father."

The instruments were brought, and the innocent, obeying Germanus, gave them to Vortigern - who blushing with shame, fled the assembly in confusion.

Razor, comb and scissors were presumably called for to tonsure the child; it is reported that Germanus made a monk of him. But was the saint implying something else in getting them passed to Vortigern? For a comb, razor and shears were the prize Arthur had to win from between the ears of the fierce Moon-boar Twrch Trwyth in the Mabinogion, and as in the tale of Sampson and Delilah, seemed to symbolise the eclipse of the sun by the moon – the sun's locks or corona apparently being sheared by the moon at the time of eclipse. Sampson means "of the sun" and Vortigern like all British kings had solar status too.

Was Germanus predicting his impending (and permanent) eclipse? I ask because our saint was out to extirpate Druidic sun-worship, as another excerpt from Nennius shows. But before relating this it is worthwhile pondering for a moment on Vortigern's Welsh name and that of his son who is familiar to us as Vortimer. They were respectively Gwetheyrn and Gwrthevir, both names strangely near Uther and Arthur, when one takes into account the Welsh aspirated G and the oo-sound of their W. There is some evidence that they were not so much names but divine titles taken by rulers, and indicating sky or solar origins. "Uther" and "Arthur" lived at just this period, if they lived at all; so it seems more than possible that Vortimer-Gwrthevir, who fought bravely against the Saxons his father had invited in and even expelled them for a time from our shores, may be the basis for the historical side of the noble Arthur. His sky-title blending with this may well have given him his Round Table, which as we have seen, "was made by Merlin to signify the round world, and the round canopy of the planets, stars and many other things." – The Zodiac!

Both Uther and Vortigern had commerce with Merlin – at least in legend, so it is probable that Gwetheyrn-Uther-Vortigern are one and the same – a character compounded of much ancient myth and a little half-remembered history. In an old poem "Marwnad Uthyr Pendragon" Uther is quite obviously an ancient god, calling himself "I, Gorlassar, the Etherial." Uther should be pronounced Ether! "Gorlassar", a name which includes that of Asser, sun-god of Asia, becomes in Malory "Gorlois, duke of Cornwall", whom Uther cuckolds with Merlin's help, thus siring Arthur on Gorlois' unsuspecting wife. It is not difficult here to see the ancient gods at play, or to conclude that Arthur was once seen as a typical sun-hero, half-human, half-divine.

Germanus was bent on destroying these sun-gods with their adulterous and incestuous habits, and trying to replace them with another set, not dissimilar. (For was the human Virgin Mary not impregnated by God Himself?) So in this last episode which Nennius represents as history, the intrepid saint confronts another "iniquitous and tyrannical king named Benlli" - undoubtedly the sun-god Beli or Belinus, or his kingly representative. But Benlli kept him waiting all day outside his city walls until Germanus lost all patience and called down fire from heaven, so that the city and all within it were burnt to death. Germanus raised up a poor man who had given him hospitality outside the city gates, called Catel Drunluc, to be king of Powys in Benlli's stead; his seed reigning there until Nennius' day.

ST GWYNNLYW (White Lion?) ap Glywys ap Tegid ap Cadell Ddyrnllug - was St Cadoc's father; and despite his resounding pedigree, something of a rogue, being addicted to brigandage and "carnal allurements". So when he asked king Brychan of Brecon for his daughter Gwladys' hand in marriage, he was not surprisingly rejected. But undeterred, he rode to Brecon with his men and carried her off. Brychan pursued them and slew some two hundred of Gwynnllyw's men, but the couple riding the same horse escaped into Glywyssing, Gwynnlyw's territory, a tract of land between the Usk and Towy rivers named after his father.

Arthur was playing dice with Cei (Kay) and Bedivere on top of a nearby hill at the time, and watched the slaughter. Being overcome with temptation for Gwladys' beauty, he proposed that they should kill Gwynnlyw and abduct her themselves. (Is this the Arthur we have come to know and love?) But to their credit, his knights cried shame on him and voted that instead they should help him as he was now inside his own borders, and fight against Brychan. This they did, and Brychan retired defeated, minus his daughter. (It is interesting to see Sir Kay emerging from this foray so untarnished).

So Gwynnlyw and Arthur are connected. But the incident that accounts for his inclusion in these pages is this.

Gwynnlyw's brigands had stolen a cow belonging to St Tathan - the only source of milk for his monastery of twelve monks. Tathan went boldly to the White Lion's den to ask for it back, but Gwynnlyw saw him from afar and decided to play a deadly trick on him. As the monk trudged up the hill he ordered a cauldron of boiling water to be placed in the hall, and covered over with reeds. When Tathan arrived he invited him to sit on this reedy seat, hoping he would fall in. But the reeds became miraculously stiff and supported the saint. Perhaps he saw steam rising from them and suspecting foul play sat gingerly on the cauldron's rim?

This apparent miracle, however, impressed Gwynnlyw, and changing his tune he returned the precious cow and invited the saint to baptise his baby son, born that very night. The magnanimous Tathan agreed to this and named the infant Cadoc.

Taking this tale literally for a moment, it seems likely enough that a cauldron of boiling water would be prepared for an imminent birth. But I suspect that the whole story was adapted to Christian times from an original which was designed to hint at a sun-king's birth; the coincidence of the cow (that recurring symbol of the earth-goddess), and the Aquarian or winter-solstice cauldron of rebirth are too redolent of Zodiacal calendar-myth. The reeds too hint at the transition from death to rebirth at water's edge; was Tathan a Christian substitute for the old sun-king, condemned to die that the new sun might be reborn?

When St Cadoc grew up, ashamed of his father's wicked ways, he converted his parents to Christianity. The rumbustious old reprobate was reluctant at first, but the gentle Gwladys persuaded him, saying "let us listen to our son, and he will be a father to us." She was of course one of the twenty-four sons and daughters of Brychan, that founder of one of the Three Holy families of Britain, most of whose offspring became saints.

Gwynnlyw and the faithful Gwladys were in the habit of going down the hill to the Usk where they bathed together naked, but now they were Christians their puritanical son put a stop to this, insisting on his mother bathing in a separate place; he found a spring of ice-cold water for her on the river-bank just above Ebbw Bridge. In Tredegar Park is a bath-house built in 1719 called the Lady's Well. She lies in a mound in the park.

Gwynnlyw, now a full-blown saint, founded a church at Newport; once St Gwynnlyw's it has now corrupted to St Woolo's. He is said to be buried there, and his fort can still be identified on Stow Hill nearby.

There is a touching account of their bathing habit in the "Cambro-British Saints". "They did not wash themselves in the frosty season of winter less than in the heat of summer; they rose from their beds in the middle of the night, and after a bath returned to their coldest apartment, put on their clothes and visited the church, praying and kneeling before the altar until day. Thus they led an eremitical life, enjoying the fruits of their labour, and taking nothing that belonged to other persons."

ST CADOC, born about 497, son of the aforesaid Gwynnlyw, was a great saint.

He is said to have founded Llancarfan monastery by seeing a wild swan nestling in a bush, while below at its roots a boar dug with its tusks, eyeing him meaningfully the while. Such symbolism was irresistible to a Celt; a place for the Holy Spirit (the swan), a Christian monastery founded on Druidic roots (the boar)?

Druids called themselves Syweddydd - swine. Most churches and monastories had such founding-myths at this period: the practice must have been inherited from Druid omen-seeking, though it was not exclusive to them, as many Greek cities and shrines were also found by following animals or birds. Perhaps it had a stratum of common-sense. Water and fertility of the land were essential to the founding of a community and animals were more likely to sense water and to rest in fertile spots than arid ones. One wonders if the magically-flowering staff of some saints was not a similar test of land-fertility - allowing a little longer for the testing-stick to bud than is reported by the old hagiographers.

St Cadoc's Life is by far the longest account we have of any Celtic saint, doubtless because it was written by Lifris, a later abbot of Llancarfan, (10th century) doing his founder proud. It is full of spectacular miracles, some quite savage; such as the occasion when Cadoc was asked to feed a hungry band of hunters in his uncle's retinue. He did so very reluctantly, having more than enough of his own hungry mouths to feed - and as soon as the hunters had swallowed their repast, the earth opened and swallowed them up in return. Hunters, Cadoc obviously felt, should be able to feed themselves. A useful tale to spread around in order to discourage marauding bands from poaching on monastery lands?

It is only fair to say that such incidents are more than made up for by innumerable miracle healings and other acts of benevolence, but there is only room here for such incidents that give a hint of the Zodiac – since that is my purpose.

Cadoc is reputed, like many other saints of his time, to have gone on pilgrimage to Jerusalem. While there he greatly admired three stone altars and wished that he might have them for his monastery, but was at a loss to know how to transport them back with him. But when he returned to Llancarfan, there they were, magically wafted across the world and waiting for him. This sounds like an echo of David's and Carantoc's altars from heaven, and thus a memory of the Glastonbury Zodiac again.

In this context it is interesting to examine St John's vision of the New Jerusalem. It was, oddly enough, a cube; the length and breadth were each 12000 furlongs, and its height was the same. There was no temple, for the Lord filled it; there were no houses, at least none were mentioned. Its single street was of gold, yet transparent as glass; the Water of Life flowed from a throne in the midst of it, and the Tree of Life somehow stood on either side of the stream, bearing twelve kinds of fruit, one for each month. Twelve pearly gates were in its four walls, three on each side. (Revelations 21.)

It is clearly not a city in the accepted sense, however heavenly, but a philosophic and mathematical scheme in the Platonic (perhaps Pythagorean) mode, a diagram of the Space-Time Cosmos and its purpose in Evolution, dealing with Time, until the end of Time. But so is the Zodiac. Much of St John's vision is astrological - the seven stars, the seven churches, etc., referring to the planets and their character. The passage where the stars fall to earth must have alerted Celtic Christians particularly to their own sacred Star-Temple on earth. The serpent with the lion on its back would have been recognisable to them as Leo rising on the back of the constellation Hydra, steeped as they were in Druidic traditions of star-lore; they would have recognised the Four Beasts as the Lion, Bull, Man of Sagittarius (whose head lies due east of the Zodiac centre) and Eagle of Aquarius as the four compass-points. (St John must have meant them as such too, for it was well after his time that the Church made these ancient geophysical symbols into the four Evangelists).

The Water of Life issuing from the throne must have reminded them irresistibly of Chalice Well Spring flowing from the Tor, especially when they read that the Tree of Life was on either side of it – for the twelve fruits or signs of the Zodiac are just so placed. Indeed it is difficult to visualise a single tree on either side of a stream in any other way. What else could St John have meant?

Yes, it is not difficult to see how the Celtic saints recognised the New Jerusalem in their own anciently sacred Avalon. St John's "throne" amid a sea of glass must have seemed to them an accurate description of the Tor, the original "Glass Castle" of folklore, reflected in and rising out of the flooding Severn waters which often surrounded it.

It has been speculated that St John was not prophesying the end of the world, but the end of a precessional Age; more – the end of a Precessional Cycle of 26000 years and the beginning of a new cycle with Christ as the Saviour of this New Dispensation. This theory has already been set forth at greater length, however, in the chapter on Joseph of Arimathea.

This grand conception may well have been a big factor in the Druidic turnover to Christianity, which, as has often been remarked, was surprisingly peaceful in Britain.

Royal St Cadoc may have been the "Cado" who in Carantoc's legend ruled Somerset with Arthur. Cadoc acquired over the ages a great reputation for wisdom, but this was partly due to confusing his sayings with the "Dicta Catonis" or Sayings of Cato, a book very popular in Europe by the 8th century. Thus Cadoc was given the title "Ddoeth", the Wise. To him who hath, more shall be given!

Here are a few of them. "There is no man a hero save him that will speak the truth. There is nothing near a man save what he cannot reach – himself. There is no loud voice save that which no-one hears – conscience. No man has sense save him that perceives he is a fool. There is no man thoughtful save him that is quiet. There is no man pious save him who is cheerful." And

"There is no God but that which can have no superior.

There is no superior but that which is superior to all.

There is nothing superior to all but Love.

There is no Love but God - no God but Love."

Asked to define Love, he said "Love is heaven". "And hate?" asked a disciple. "Hate is hell." "And conscience?" "Conscience is the eye of God in man."

(Most of these come from The Cambrian Register, vol. 3, translated by Thomas ap Jevan.) There are enough of Cadoc's sayings to fill a good-sized book. He became so famous for wise saws that everything of that kind in the Welsh language became attributed to his name, and thus, says the Myvyrian Archaeology, "the fame of Cadoc swallowed up that of everyone else."

These saints were well-read, not only in the bible, but the classics. There are two stories of Cadoc's books, lost in the waves, but returned by a fish. This one suspects was the Zodiac's Salmon of Wisdom! Cadoc loved Virgil, and one day walking by the sea with his friend Gildas (also called the Wise) with his Virgil under his arm, the subject came up of whether Virgil, being a pagan, was in Hell. "Of course he is" said Gildas, a somewhat ferocious and dogmatic Christian. Cadoc was not so sure. Just then a gust of wind blew the book into the sea. Cadoc was deeply upset, and mourned its loss, which seemed to confirm Gildas' harsh judgement. Retiring to his cell he resolved not to eat or drink until "he knew truly what fate God has allotted to those who sang upon earth as the angels sing in heaven." Dreaming, he heard a soft voice say "Pray for me, pray for me, and I shall yet sing eternally the mercy of the Lord." The next day his Virgil was "magically and wonderfully returned to him".

Another time, returning from a meditation on one of the islands in the Severn much favoured by these saints for Lenten fasts, he found his disciples had failed to pack his Enchiridion and left it behind. Furious, he cursed the two offenders and sent them back far across the Severn, saying "Go, and may you never return!" This was irrational to say the least, if he wanted his book back. They set out in their coracle, but on the way back it capsized and both monks and the precious book were drowned. (One of them, the unfortunate Barruc, has named Barry Island.) Unmoved apparently by this tragedy and hungry after his long fast, Cadoc ordered a supper of salmon, and when it was caught and opened there of course was his precious Enchiridion, its cover completely dry and unstained.

As the book was lost in the Severn, there can be no doubt that it was the Salmon of Wisdom who sacrificed himself to recover it. And as even to touch him and lick one's finger brought enlightenment, we may infer that Cadoc's repast was the source of his sapient reputation. It happened to him twice, so he became doubly wise.

Whether Cadoc was the Cato who ruled Somerset with Arthur or not, he is certainly connected with him in the later Welsh Triads, where he is lauded as "One of the Three Knights of upright Judgement" of Arthur's Court, being more concerned with righting the wrongs of widows, orphans and strangers and with religion and equity than the other two. He was also One of the Three Chaste Knights of Arthur, One of the Three Holy Bachelors of Britain, and One of the Three Wise Men who counselled Arthur. His exalted reputation has in fact roused speculation as to whether he is the original Sir Galahad - who for all his perfection was, like Cadoc, not above a little mass-slaughter and mayhem when the occasion seemed to demand it.

Cadoc's enormous vitality took him to Ireland where he helped to revive the church which was failing after the death of St Patrick: to Brittanny, and to Scotland where he was invited by Marc Conomanus, king of Strathclyde, to build a monastery. Leaving Gildas in charge of Llancarfan, he found a site at Carmunnock in the Cathkin Hills. He began to dig, and uncovered some enormous bones; so large was the arched collar-bone that a horse and cart could easily have been driven underneath it.

Cadoc prayed to be told whose they were; at once a giant appeared, claiming them as his – he had been a king in the north who for his robberies and marauding forays had been consigned to Hell; his name was Caw of Prydyn. Could he use his great strength helping Cadoc dig the monastery's foundations? That way he would earn remission of his sentence. Cadoc gladly accepted this human bulldozer, and the work proceeded apace.

Baring-Gould in his Lives of the British Saints speculates that Cadoc had unwittingly exhumed the bones of King Caw, who was Gildas' father, and was at one time a great man in Strathclyde; and that Cadoc built his monastery over the grave as a compliment to Gildas. The similarity of the name Caw to Cawr, a giant, accounted he thought for Caw's vastly increased stature. But would Cadoc spread a tale that made his friend's father a robber and a rogue? Caw was if not quite a saint, at all events the founding-father of one of the Three Saintly Families of Britain; his father Geraint down in Cornwall was well-known for his Christian sympathies and benefactions; nor would Caw's large family of sons and daughters, all fervent Christians, be pleased to hear their father had been in Hell.

Nor is it likely that King Caw, Gildas father, was buried in Scotland; he is thought to have been a soldier with the Romans on the Wall, who soon after the Roman army left in 410 fled to Anglesey with his family, being given land there by Maelgwyn king of Gwynnedd, on which he built his tribal monastery.

No. I submit that the tale is a parable, as usual. Cadoc I suspect was building Christianity in Strathclyde's Druidic centre, and using the strength of the Glastonbury Giant Cawr to help him adapt from the old faith to the new. Lot of Lothian was an Arthurian. Merddin the Bard, fleeing to Clydebank, was writing his lament "Avallenau" for Avalon's lost mysteries there. And one has only to recall such names as Helland, Hellyar and Hellard on Somerset's Dog to see that Caw or Cawr had indeed come from "Hell". Patrick too had the help of a disinterred giant. He too it seems built on the foundation of the Glastonbury Giants.

St EDEYRN is said in the Iolo MSS to have been a son of Vortigern, by incest with his own daughter. Despite this inauspicious beginning, or perhaps because of it, he became a saint in St Cadoc's monastery and later founded his own at Llanedeyrn on the Rumney near Cardiff, where he lies buried. But Nennius tells us that Vortigern's incestuous son was St Faustus who was adopted by St Germanus and became bishop of Riez, Brittany, and doesn't mention a son named Edeyrn at all. And if Faustus was a Latin name for Welsh Edeyrn he could not have been a pupil of St Cadoc, who was born about 50 years later, c497.

So St Edeyrn is a very shadowy figure. But his name reverberates from the pagan past, and the few incidents and characteristics remembered about him seem to belong to a Celtic god or demi-god rather than a Christian saint. Older accounts make him a bard, and like Gwyn, a son of Nudd, of the family of Maelgwyn Gwynedd. But Nudd, whether male or female, whether Neith the fate-spinner or Nodens the Romano-British fisher-god or Llud the sun-god (expert opinions are divided) was a Celtic deity, who hunted dying souls in the wind with a pack of red-eared "wish-hounds" to bring them to Annwn. Gwyn as we have seen was Lord of Glastonbury Tor, thus a Glastonbury Giant. Edeyrn I suspect was originally another.

A St Edeyrn is remembered in Brittany, pictured at Lannedern and Plogonnec near Douarnenez, riding on a stag. This unusual pose is accounted for by relating that he saved the stag from hunters, and that the animal became his inseparable companion; but has led some to identify him with Cernunnos the Celtic Nature god. And certainly St Edeyrn hid himself away as a hermit in the depths of the forest. He saved the stag from being torn to pieces by hounds; the former brother of Gwyn of the Wild Hunt has become the Christian wild-life protector!

Herne the stag-horned Hunter of Windsor Forest is undoubtedly the same primaeval Nature-god as Cernunnos; he too had a pack of Hell-hounds which can still occasionally be heard baying in the wind of wintry nights.

Edeyrn ap Nudd has not only infiltrated Celtic Christianity, he also appears in Arthurian legend as a knight of more than ordinary stature. Aloof, arrogant and sombre, he brings his godlike aura with him. Arthur commands him to kill no less than "three most atrocious giants" of Brenteknol, so he must have been one himself. He does kill them, but dies in the endeavour. Arthur, finding him stretched out on the ground (like a true Glastonbury Giant) weeps at his loss and has masses said for him, whereupon Edeyrn comes to life again like the Nature-god he is. To find the two brother-giants occupying these two prominent hills in the Zodiac area is surely significant. Brent Knoll, though not in its circle, is within a giant's shout of Gwyn's Tor.

Yet this superhuman knight is at last overcome by the valiant young Gereint of Cornwall in a tournament for a silver sparrow-hawk. Edeyrn has already won it twice and if he wins a third time he will gain the coveted title of "The knight of the Sparrow-hawk". Is this brother Gwyn's Aquarian Eagle?

But young Gereint wrests victory from him, and bending over his prostrate body sword in hand demands to know Edeyrn 's best-kept secret - his name. He admits it only on pain of death, is spared and sent back to Arthur's court to tell his sorry tale. But Arthur is very relieved to have him back and nurses him back to health. In his Mabinogion tale it is worth noting that the mysterious Edeyrn is first encountered in the depths of the forest while Gereint in the queen's company is hunting a stag. And is Edeyrn's return from death in the encounter with the giants a hint that the Glastonbury Giants are revived as Arthur's knights?

Two other equally obscure Welsh saints, Sts. Edi and Edren, may be aliases of Edeyrn. St Edi lived in a giant's cave called Ogor Cawr at Llanedi, Carmarthen, and was reputedly of great stature; Baring Gould who records him says that this is clearly pagan myth Christianised, and the church is now dedicated to St Edith. But when the "British Saints" was written (1908) the giant's bed and seat were still being pointed out, and if this is no longer true, magnificent views from the cave-mouth will still reward the pilgrim.

Nothing is known now of St Edren, whose Church near St Davids is now given to St Lawrence; but a strange superstition attached itself to his churchyard. The grass there was long held to cure those who had been bitten by mad dogs. Folk used to cut it and spread it on bread and butter. As Browne Willis records the church as Llanedern, dedicated to St Edern, it certainly seems possible that the saint was held to repair the ravages of Gwyn's or Herne's Wild Hunt-pack, as the Breton St Edeyrn was reputed to have done.

One more speculation. As the knight Edeyrn occurs in Chretien de Troyes as Yder, is it possible that Edeyrn was once Idris of Cader Idris? Idris is listed in the Triads as One of the Three Happy Astronomers of Britain. Gwyn ap Nudd was another. But Druid astronomers were also astrologers, highly valued advisers of kings for their knowledge of the Cosmos and Man's place and purpose in it. Techniques for changing consciousness were employed in their Mysteries, and it was said that he who dared to spend a night on Cader Idris'mountain-top would be found in the morning either dead, mad or inspired.

So does my tentative identification of Edeyrn with Idris not cast him in a very different role from that of the horned Nature-Giant of the wildwood? Are they not too incompatible to be fused? Not so, if we enrol Idris-Edeyrn among Glastonbury's Nature -Giants, its Temple of the Stars. As Gwyn ap Nudd said long ago of his dog Dormarth (who is surely the Zodiac's Girt Dog of Langport) "Handsome is my dog, and round-bodied. Dormarth with the ruddy nose, ground-grazing; how you gaze on me when I mark your wanderings on cloud-mount." He belonged in other words to both earth and sky, the ruddy nose being Sirius the dog-star. But dogs don't have red noses. The Girt Dog of Langport, does, however. For his nose is the great mound of Burrow Mount at Athelney, which is made of red earth. The two brother-astronomers, Ider and Gwyn of the Tor, should in any case be Glastonbury Giants. Early names for Gemini's Twins?

St Edeyrn

CHAPTER 7

St KEYNE, CAIN or CEINWEN, Virgin, c450?

As my maternal ancestors have lived for uncounted generations in and around the Cornish village of St Keyne, and as when my own branch moved away they formed the nostalgic habit of naming their houses after their saint for three generations, her name was familiar to me from an early age. But it was not until I began to be magnetised by the Glastonbury Zodiac and found Keinton Mandeville on Virgo's hand holding her wheatsheaf that it dawned on me that she might be a pre-Christian goddess canonised. Haddon and Stubbs say in fact that there is no reliable evidence that she ever existed at all, and another hagiographer (Rees?) noting the ubiquity of ancient dedications to her assumes her to have been too energetic to have been a woman, and supposes St Keyne to have been a man!

John of Tynemouth's legend however makes her one of the daughters of Brychan King of Brecon, whose children, twelve sons and twelve daughters, mostly became saints. But the list of their names is variable, and seems to be a refuge for Celtic deities who by popular demand have crept into the Christian calendar. Non, mother of St David, Yse and Mabena were her sisters, these last being suspiciously like pre-Christian names for the young Son of the Sun. And St Non or Nun herself is so overlaid with Mother-Goddess myth that her historic personality is almost smothered,

The word Cain in Welsh means "bright, shining, beautiful" and sometimes she shone like the sun, sometimes appeared as white as shining snow. This alone makes one suspect a deity. Her beauty attracted many suitors, but determined to be a bride of Christ, she fled from Brecon across the Severn to what is now Keynsham to beg from the local lord enough land to build an anchorite's cell. He gave her a snake-infested wood, but she surmounted this problem by turning all the serpents to stone - which sufficiently accounts for the prevalence of ammonites in the area. (St Hilda performed the same miracle at Whitby).

At some time she settled at St Keyne near Liskeard, and here she blessed her holy well in truly matriarchal style by ordaining that couples married in her church should race a mile downhill to her well as soon as the ring was on, and that the first to drink the water should wear the trousers ever after.

Southey's poem "The Well of St Keyne" records the ingenuity of one such bride in the words of her luckless swain -

> I hastened as soon as the wedding was done
> And left my wife in the porch
> But i'faith, she had been wiser than me
> For she took a bottle to church!

My cousin Jane Clemens who lived at the Churchtown farm assured me that couples there still run to the well as energetically as they ever did.

St Keyne went to St Michael's Mount, where her nephew St Cadoc is said to have visited her, and where the topmost tower of the castle is remembered as her seat. The same tale is told, that anyone who dares to sit there poised giddily above the sea will thereafter be the master in the marriage.

But this was before the cult of St Michael took hold of Cornwall. There is some evidence that the Mount was earlier called Dinsol - fort of the Sun, and this westernmost part of the peninsula was once called Belerion. The sun-god Bel was once worshipped here. Was St Keyne, before she was enrolled amongst the saints, his consort? Was she the Earth-mother, ever Virgin, who named all Cornwall - Kerin - as her cornucopia-horn? Was Liskeard her court? For one of its early forms was Liskered, meaning perhaps Ceredwen's Hall. Was she a snake-goddess after the Cretan pattern? Certainly the number of dedications to her in the west suggest an ancient widespread cult; she is patroness of Llangein, Carmarthen, of Kentchurch, Herefordshire (new dedicated to the Virgin Mary); Llangeinor, Glamorgan; two places in Anglesey, Llangeinwen and Cerrig Ceinwen, and there is a Ffynnon Gain at Bletherston, Pembroke; in Cornwall are Kenwyn, Truro, and a chapel at East Looe, now given to St Anne - who is herself remembered as a Cornish or Breton Princess, mother of the Virgin Mary, and thus a suspect Celtic goddess in origin.

John of Tynemouth tells how her nephew Cadoc persuaded St Keyne to return at last to Wales, where at the foot of a great mountain she caused a healing spring to flow. Just before she died she said to him that the place would fall into the hands of sinful men, whom she would root out and lead thither others who would find her tomb, so the name of the Lord would be blessed there for ever.

If St Keyne is Virgo's snake-goddess, it is interesting that two serpents surround Virgo in the sky - Hydra whose tiny stars meander past her, and Draco the circumpolar dragon, whose heads can be traced on the ground near her in the Zodiac's centre. Guin-Eve is still being tempted by the serpent Draco round the Pole-star Tree of Knowledge with his Avalon apples of Wisdom.

But some of my reasons for identifying St Keyne with an archetypal goddess border on the weird, involving strange coincidences.

There was the occasion when I saw a dead but undamaged snake on the road while travelling from Keinton Mandeville to Keynsham in pursuit of the elusive saint. I picked it up and put it in the car as a useful adjunct to my art classes. At Keynsham we found that the church was dedicated to St John, and calling at the vicarage to protest were given a leaflet on St Keyne; it was then (with the snake in the car) that we read for the first time how our intrepid virgin had turned Keynsham's snakes to stone. We were told that she probably never existed, as Keynsham was spelt Cainesham in Domesday Book. My married name! My husband and I looked at each other incredulously; it was becoming difficult to agree that she never existed - she seemed very much alive. Never before or since have I found a dead snake to take home.

Then there was the time when making a film of the Zodiac we went to Gatwick to discuss with the pilot how high we had to fly to get Virgo's head and wheatsheaf together on one shot (she is four miles long), and how to avoid intruding on HMS Heron's airspace, which at Yeovilton is very near her head. Thirsty after this long discussion we called at the Queens's Head at Bolney, on our way to Brighton for the day. Imagine our amazement to find the bar festooned with miniature corn-dollies! There were more types of corn represented in this collection than I'd ever heard of, and we were told that it was the immemorial custom here for farmers to present a new one at each harvest. It certainly seemed that Old Mother Carey - Ceredwen Ogiervran Amhad – "Goddess of various seeds" as the old Celts called her – was showing us just how various her seeds could be, and was bent on making her archetypal presence felt. We noted some intriguing place-names nearby: Skaynes Hill and Keymer, and wondered whether her cult was not widespread over Britain before the Saxons chased her and the Britons into the west.

This extraordinary piece of Jungian synchronicity happened about 1970; Alas, when I visited the Queen's head a year ago both landlord and corndollies were gone, and when I followed up the new address I was given it turned out to be a false trail. Another charming old custom swept into oblivion.

2nd-3rd Century Carving Coventina's Wall
Higher Rochester, Northumberland

THE THREE EVES OF EVESHAM

The first founding-legend of Evesham's once-magnificent abbey that I came across was to the effect that three devout ladies, all named Eve, came to St Egwin bishop of Worcester about the year 700, wishing to take the veil, and that in consequence he founded the abbey of Evesham.

One had to wonder whether these ladies were not the ancient Goddess in Christian guise - the goddess of the 3-phased moon, of earth, sky and sea, the Mother of All in her threefold aspect of Virgin, Mother and all-wise hag.

But visiting Evesham when opportunity allowed, I was told a somewhat different version, namely that Eova or Eoves, Bishop Egwin's swineherd, had a vision of three ladies among the leaves as he minded his pigs in the forest. Two of them were unnamed, but the central figure was that of the Virgin. On the spot where this vision occurred Egwin built Evesham's first shrine, and fired with religious zeal, padlocked his leg to a heavy beam, threw the key into the Avon, and thus shackled set out on a pilgrimage to Rome. After long and arduous journeying he reached the Holy City, and hungering, caught a fish in the Tiber. Within it, needless to say, was the lost key to his padlock. His faith had won him his freedom.

It was Eofa, not Eve, I was assured, who had named Evesham. So popular did this vision make Egwin's shrine that it grew over the centuries into a magnificent monastery with two churches beside the abbey.

These still survive, though the abbey was razed to the ground after the Dissolution, leaving only a beautiful bell-tower and an expanse of greensward. Nevertheless the whole complex is still impressive, and with the wealth of half-timbered buildings around it, Evesham is still worthy of a pilgrimage for those who need to travel into the past.

The town's founding-legend has it seems undergone several changes over the centuries. One suspects that the padlocked beam and its key found in the Tiber's fish were added later by Roman Churchmen to remind those of their congregation who still clung to Celtic Christianity that true freedom could only be obtained by St Peter's key. I suspect too that the Hwicci or Gewissae (whose land this was) worshipped the Triple Goddess in pagan times, and that it was indeed she who named the town. It was called Eves-homme already in 709, when Egwin was building his church and dedicating it to the Blessed Virgin. Why then was the place not named Marychurch or something like it?

I surmise that the name Eve was chosen to placate the traditional worshippers of the "Mothers" of Celtic times, who protected all wells, springs and small rivers. It was at least biblical, and was sufficiently like the Saxon ae, aewille (spring, water) to bridge the transition from the old faith to the new. Evesham is very watery, being situated in a U-bend of the Avon; Eofa's vision of three ladies makes it very probable that the Triple Goddess was worshipped there. His name is suspiciously like Eve, and must have been pronounced identically; is it not more likely the name Eofa was given him after his vision, in recognition of his special relationship with the local goddesses? Or even (horrid thought!) that the saintly Egwin made up the whole tale in order to wean the Hwicci of the district from pagan goddess-worship to Christianity? The transition is complete in the stained-glass window of the parish church, where the Blessed Virgin alone looks down upon the adoring swineherd; but the original triad is preserved in another window in neighbouring St Lawrence's church.

The goddess has as many names as the tribes who held her sacred; hills were her breasts, and the life-giving streams issuing from them were "Liebfraumilch". The Seine was named after her as Sequana, the Marne recalled the Matronae, the Severn commemorated the nymph Sabrina, the Thames became the Isis, Queen of triple goddesses, at Oxford, and the many Yeo rivers derive from Eve or Gifl, the Giver or all good gifts to men. All yeomen are her husbandmen. She has certainly blessed the Vales of Avalon and Evesham with fruitful orchards; but how have her yeomen requited her? By naming her the mother of all Evil.

Yeoveney near Staines in Middlesex was once spelt Yevenay, and in earlier times Giueneya – reminding us that Guinevere had Eve in her name; it can be translated as "White or Shining Eve". Is it coincidence merely that she was accused (though falsely) of giving one of Arthur's knights a poisoned apple? Guinevere's father was Leodegrance, king of Camelot; his name makes him Virgo's neighbouring effigy of Leo. Cadbury Castle, the traditional Camelot, guards Virgo-Guinevere from the south-east and must long have been regarded as their stronghold. Leodegrance gave the Round Table (the Somerset Zodiac) to Arthur as her marriage dowry – though matriarchally speaking, it was hers to give. It must be in her honour that the village of Queen Camel so near Virgo's effigy belonged for centuries to successive queens of England. Her triple aspect is clearly seen in the Three Queens who attended Arthur's funeral-barge.

Robert Graves in his "White Goddess" asserts that the Greek tale of the Judgement of Paris arose from iconotropy – in other words, some ancient enemy of Womankind misconstrued an old carving of three ladies, a shepherd, and an apple passing between them, as Paris judging Aphrodite the fairest by handing her the apple; thus sowing jealousy between the ladies by the "Apple of Discord".

Not so, says Graves. "To award an apple to the Love-Goddess would have been an impertinence on the shepherd's part. All apples were hers. Did Adam give the Mother of All Living an apple?" No, the apple was going the other way; the Triple Goddess in the original icon was not only giving Mankind the fruits of the earth – she was inspiring him towards immortality by love of her beauty.

Hercules too, Graves reminds us, was given Three Golden Apples of Wisdom by the Three Daughters of the West from the orchard-Garden of the Hesperides. The old geographer Ptolemy calls Hartland Point on the Devon-Somerset border "Heracles Akron". Not far from the Zodiac! Another Greek account states that Hercules travelled from Greece through Illyria up the river Po to reach the Hesperides - a bee-line for Britain. And as it was these apples that made Hercules immortal, it begins to look as if he came to learn Druidic wisdom from its Somerset source.

Druids were a self-deprecating lot, calling themselves Gadflies (perhaps to indicate that they stung their pupils into wakefulness) – or Syweddydd, "swine", perhaps to say that they dug for the truffles of Truth from the Earth Herself, or because the many-breasted sow was a favourite form taken by the fecund Mother. So Eofa the swineherd may be a code-word for something else. Swineherds have often been credited with founding holy places – Glastonbury itself has a legend that a Saxon, Glaesting, followed his sow many miles until she settled there and farrowed, contentedly munching the apples of Avalon; Bath was founded by the swineherd Bladud; and Braunton in Devon still displays its founding sow and her piglets on an old bench-end in its church; they showed St Brannoc the site when he sailed from Wales in the 6th century in a stone coffin.

May it not be that these places remember an earlier priesthood than Christianity; one that held the Goddess and her Mysteries in awe?

ST URSULA. Geoffrey of Monmouth's History of the Kings of Britain gives the tragic tale of St Ursula and her 11000 martyred virgins, though it is only one of many versions, for her cult was enormously popular in the Middle ages. He makes her the beautiful daughter of Dinotus duke of Cornwall, much desired in marriage by Cornish Conan Meriadoc, governor of Brittany. In the 380s Conan was a claimant to the throne of Britain, but to his chagrin another was chosen, Maximian, an able soldier part British part Roman by descent (hardly a surprising choice as Britain at the time was in Roman hands). But Maximian, the "Prince Macsen" of the

Mabinogion, had greater ambitions, and with Conan as his lieutenant denuded Britain of all its fighting men in a continental campaign to become Emperor of Rome. This aim he briefly achieved by murdering the reigning emperor, though he was himself assassinated only nine months later.

Maximian, known to historians as Magnus Clemens Maximus, compensated his faithful lieutenant Conan for this service by awarding him Brittany, and his soldiers settled there in great numbers, thus robbing Britain of all its defenders – an opportunity that Picts, Saxons and Irish, seized with both hands. Geoffrey of Monmouth castigates Maximian roundly for putting personal ambition before the defence of the country of which he had been chosen king.

Conan thus found himself settling the colony of "Little Britain" and sent to Duke Dinotus in Cornwall for the beautiful Ursula, asking him to provide wives for his soldiers also to the tune of 11000 virgins of noble birth and 60000 more "of common birth". This tall order was duly executed by the obliging Dinotus who scoured the land for them, and without asking their consent packed them into a fleet of ships which sailed down the Thames into the Channel. But alas! once out to sea a contrary wind "blew up in their teeth," scattering them; many ships foundered and the rest were blown on to "barbarous islands" (presumably the Hook of Holland or the German coast) where they were propositioned by the Huns "who would fain have wantoned with them, but meeting denial, fell upon them and slaughtered by far the most part of them without mercy". Moreover when the Huns learnt that Britain was drained of its soldiers leaving none but "witless tillers of the soil" to defend it, they invaded in great numbers, "sacking and ravaging the cities and provinces as if they had been so many sheepfolds".

Geoffrey has placed Ursula's tale in Britain's darkest hour, interweaving it with the beginning of the withdrawal of the Imperial Legions from our shores. As it stands the story sounds most improbable, but as Magnus Maximus did indeed drain Britain of its men, leaving a surplus of eligible damsels, many may have sought emigration to redress the balance of the sexes.

One version of the tale centres on the massacre at Cologne, where the unhappy ladies are still remembered as sailing down the Rhine to their death. In fact Ursula's legend is first recorded in a sermon preached at Cologne in 800. A variant of the myth tells how Ursula made conditions before consenting to marry Conan; first , that he should become a Christian. When he consented she made another, that she and her reluctant ladies should be allowed to sail the seas for three years before their weddings, enjoying their virginal state while they may – conditions which sound suspiciously like Christianisation of earlier pagan myth. So it is interesting to find that the Gothic moon-goddess Hörstel also sailed the blue heavenly seas in her crescent moon-boat in search of a husband. Hörstel (whose name closely resembles Ursula's) lived in the Hörselberg surrounded by 1000 maidens. Tacitus testifies to the age of these beliefs, saying that "part of the Suevi (Swabians) sacrificed to Isis, her symbol a ship. This custom was brought from abroad."

It was an ancient custom in the Rhineland and Thuringia to draw a boat on wheels through the towns, accompanied by orgiastic revels which the pious monks who record this, shrink from describing in detail.

It begins to look as if St Ursula derives her legend from pagan moonmyth – her attendant virgins the countless stars. And significantly, among Ursula's virgins were twelve all called Babyla (Babylon being a synonym for star-worship), while two others were named Martha and Saula. "Merten und Seelen" – spirits and souls – suggests Baring-Gould, who subscribes to Ursula's stellar and lunar origins. He also suspects that the notion that they sailed from England is a confusion with Engel-land of the Angles, and ascribes Indo-Aryan origins for these starry spirits, which he equates with the Sanskrit Maruts.

The tale was widespread across northern Europe; a Nordic variant occurs in the Saga of Olaf Trygvasonr written by the monk Oddr in the 1100s. Here Ursula becomes Sunnifa, beautiful daughter of an Irish King, who was so desired by an ardent Viking that he put all Ireland to the flames until he obtained her. But Sunnifa, her brother Alban and many virgins all left Ireland to save it from further devastation, sailing east and trusting in God. Landing on Selja off Norway they would all have been massacred by king Hako had not the rocks opened and let them in, echoing the Pied Piper of Hamelin. They were never seen again as the rocks closed on them for ever. Despite this their relics were taken from Selja to Bergen by the devout bishop Paul!

In the late Middle Ages the curious custom appeared of founding communities of men and women called "the Skiffs of St Ursula"; these were granted special indulgences by popes. Hörstel may be dead but she wouldn't lie down, it seems; the Church often compounded with persistent and popular pagan customs by such methods. But not all popes thought that way, and sceptical Benedict XIV tried to suppress Ursula's cult altogether.

Ursula's name is not without starry significance, being Latin for the Little Bear, a constellation containing the Pole Star and sailing continually round it in the heavens as on a pivot. Was this and not the moon Ursula's boat? Ursula's symbol is a dove and in the Glastonbury Zodiac the stars of the Great Bear (presumably Ursula's heavenly father) fall on the Libran Dove round Barton St David. The Great Bear's two pointer stars point always to the Pole Star. One is tempted to wonder whether Hörstel derives from Ursula rather than vice versa, as has been assumed so far –for her father was the Sky-god Niordr, and what can that mean but "the North"?

Have we here a fragment of Druidic Zodiac myth? Is Ursula the ever-virgin May-Queen celebrated still at Minehead and Padstow by the Hobby-Horse Boat? Ceridwen her Welsh alias presided over calendrical Mysteries which involved initiates in an ordeal of near-drowning and rebirth (Ursula's starry spirits and souls Merten und Seelen or Martha and Saula). This terrifying ordeal was undergone voluntarily by brave candidates in a consciousness-raising experience, as a Druidic fragment records.

The novice: "Though I love the sea-beach, I dread the open sea; a billow may come undulating over the stone." Gwyddno the Hierophant replies: "To the brave, the magnanimous, the amiable, the generous one who boldly embarks, the ascending stones of the bards will prove the harbour of life." Novice: "Though I love the strand, I dread the wave. Great has been its violence, dismal the overwhelming stroke. Even to him who survives it will be the subject of lamentation. "Gwyddno tries to reassure him: "It is a pleasant act to wash in the bosom of the fair water. Though it fill the receptacle it will not disturb the heart. My associated train regard not its overwhelming. As for him who repents of this enterprise, the lofty wave has hurried the babbler far away to his death; but the brave, the magnanimous, will find his compensation in arriving safe at the stones. The conduct of the water will declare thy merit." Gwyddno rejects this pusillanimous candidate with scorn; "Thy coming without external purity is a pledge that I will not receive thee. Take out the gloomy one! My revenge upon the shoal of earthworms is their hopeless longing for the pleasant place. Out of the receptacle which is thine aversion did I obtain the rainbow".

Taliesin the Bard claims to be a successful initiate in these Mysteries –indeed, owing his inspiration to his "rebirth". Speaking of Ceridwen the dark goddess who pursues him, shape-shifting in true Celtic style, he exclaims "I fled in the form of a grain of wheat – she caught me in her fangs. In appearance she was as large as a proud mare – which she also resembled. Then was she swelling out like a ship upon the waters. Into the sea she cast me. It was an auspicious day for me when she happily suffocated me. God the Lord set me free."

As we have seen, in the Glastonbury Zodiac Cancer's maternal sign is not a Crab but the ship Argo Navis which cradles a baby - the reborn Taliesin. Argo Navis is Cancer's near neighbour in the constellations. Hörstel's father Niordr lived in heavenly Noatun. Noah's ark? And was Hörstel herself a horse – or proud mare? The Noah story is also a legend of death by drowning and rebirth on a worldwide scale – a purification by baptism of the whole human race.

One can well see how the snapping jaws of the Hobby-Horse symbolically snatched the novice to dunk him in the sea; baptism with a vengeance! The dark covering-canopy of the Horse may also have symbolised the night sky, from whence the starry spirits dropped down into the watery womb in reincarnation – a concept embraced by the Druids, as by their Indo-Aryan cousins in the east.

As these parallels between Ursula's legend and Druidic rites and teaching emerge, it is interesting to observe that most forms of her tale see her as sailing either from western Britain or Ireland to the Nordic east, and at a very early period. It seems as if the Skiffs of St Ursula may have taken cosmic Druid teachings with them and spread them abroad in Germany and Scandinavia with lasting effect. Even the apparently indigenous Hörstel's name may have starry significance in its own right as Urs-stel, or Bear stars, and not just as a corruption of Ursula. The H in her name may have been added to give the name extra meaning to Angles, Saxons and Danes, for our word horse is of Anglo-Saxon origin.

Was the Ship of Fools, so popular in mediaeval art, a sarcastic ecclesiastical comment on the Skiffs of St Ursula?

ST DUNSTAN. c 910-988. Though more a Saxon than a Celtic saint and at least three centuries later than the main Celtic saintly flowering, he deserves a place in this anthology not only because he was born in the centre of the Zodiac at Baltonsborough, educated at Glastonbury Abbey and became abbot there, but chiefly because his main legends reflect uncannily its eastern figures from Virgo through to Sagittarius, on whose broad shoulders he was born. He is remembered also at several places on the Kingston Zodiac; one wonders indeed if he chose Kingston too as the place to crown several Saxon kings in order to commemorate its ancient sanctity.

Dunstan, educated at Glastonbury Abbey and a fervent reader in its magnificent and ancient library, can hardly have failed to be acquainted with the royal Secret, especially as his father Heorstan was descended from the Wessex Royal House. Dunstan's love of learning and music puts him in the Bardic tradition which still lingered in that ancient Celtic centre.

His monkish biographer writing about 1000 AD, tells how he "loved the old heathen songs and legends" carrying his harp on his back wherever he went.

In fact he studied, played and sang so hard that he fell ill. But his talents (and no doubt his noble birth) brought him to the notice of Athelstan, who summoned him to court and showed him great favour. This of course roused the envy of less talented courtiers and he was accused of sorcery, of winning praise and affection by magic spells. He had a particular way with animals too, which was also put down to magic. He seems to have been very much in the Druidic tradition. His outstanding gifts were soon too much for his young colleagues, who when Athelstan's back was turned threw him into a muddy pond and drove him away from the court. After another grave illness he decided to become a Benedictine monk, living in a cell just high enough to stand up and long enough to lie down. At this time he became an excellent metal-worker, and the story is told that one day as he was heating his metal in a furnace the Devil appeared in the doorway, as a lovely lady, taunting him. (Dunstan was at that time wrestling with his ardent nature, trying to come to terms with the celibate life of a monk). After a while he could stand the diabolical temptations no longer and heating the tongs to red-hot he gripped the devil's nose with them until he yelled and begged for mercy, and promised to trouble him no more. Scorpio? Its metal is iron. Scorpio is the diabolical sign and the sign of sexual temptation and magnetism; the tongs perhaps symbolised Scorpio's iron claws.

When Dunstan was a boy he was friendly with a wealthy and pious lady, St Elfleda, who lived near him east of Glastonbury. She was a widow, the aunt of King Athelstan, and apparently had a widow's cruse, for when the king and his entourage came to stay her barrel of beer never failed, despite the well-known fact that Saxons are heavy drinkers. Such an archetypal widow points to Virgo, who in Arthurian legend is always the Widow Lady.

When she was dying Dunstan went to visit her and was passed on the way by a white dove, its wings flashing gold in the setting sun. When he arrived he heard her talking to someone behind the bed-curtains, and waited. Conversation ceased but no-one emerged, so Dunstan went in, but saw no-one except the dying widow. "Who were you talking to?" he asked. "Why do you ask?" she replied. "Surely with him whom you saw flying this way."

Is this not the Libran Dove, the bird of the Holy Spirit, flying towards Virgo in our Zodiac?

There is another legend involving the Dove that is transmitted locally; it is said that Dunstan was baptised in the River Brue at Tootle Bridge. As the Brue here defines the eastern wing of Libra's Dove, this tale raises Biblical images of the Baptism in Jordan, with the Logos-Dove hovering overhead. If this is not a piece of local history remembered for over a thousand years it may well have grown from local knowledge of this aerial figure in the landscape. Either way it is singularly apt. Apt too is the little bridge over the Brue at the bridge of Sagittarius' nose, nearby. Dunstan incidentally is said to have engineered much irrigation round here; the reach of the Brue drawing the Dove's wing is known as Dunstan's Dyke.

Baltonsborough Flights is another curiously apt place-name here, at the point where the stream defining the forehead of Sagittarius the sun-god cascades down a little waterfall – a flight of steep stone steps – into the wing of the Dove. The Flight of the spirit of Bel the dying sun of winter, escaping like life-blood into the spirit-Dove? Was that what St Elfleda meant?

The last legend that reads like a clue to the Zodiac tells how Dunstan, banished from court yet again by jealousy, was reinstated by Edmund. The king hunted a deer near Cheddar Gorge and was in danger of being carried over the steep cliff-edge to his death when he remembered the wrongs Dunstan had suffered, and bargaining desperately with the Lord promised that if He would stop his horse in mid-career he would reinstate the much-maligned saint. The horse miraculously stopped at the very edge of the cliff, and Edmund true to his bargain went straight to Glastonbury and proclaimed Dunstan its abbot from that moment. He also recalled him to court and belatedly recognising the saint's visionary statesmanship made him his chief adviser – an inspired choice which was continued under Edmund's brother and successor Edred after Edmund's untimely death.

The bolting horse and its half-unseated rider is strangely reminiscent of the figure of Sagittarius in our Zodiac. Can it be merely coincidence that all these legends illustrate so well the figures from Virgo to Sagittarius – or is Dunstan's biographer writing in code?

It is perhaps significant that although Dunstan's very active political life took him across southern England from west to east, these legends all refer to the Glastonbury area.

It is curious too how Sagittarian was Dunstan's meteoric career. Born on the sign, it carried him high, but at least three times threw him to the ground. Sagittarius is accident-prone. It is also menaced continually (especially in our Zodiac) by the envious claws of Scorpio; this was certainly a recurring factor in Dunstan's career. One such occasion occurred when he crowned Edred's nephew Edwy. An irresponsible boy of sixteen, Edwy deeply offended the assembled nobles by leaving them all for the company of Aelgifu his fiancee and her scheming mother, tossing off his crown in contempt. Dunstan was promptly despatched to drag him back to the ceremony (doubtless no-one else dared) and returned him forcibly to the scandalised assembly. For this he was banished yet again by the furious Edwy, who confiscated all his property and drove the long-suffering saint abroad.

He returned four years later on Edwy's convenient death, recalled at once by Edgar, Edwy's brother and successor, and began the great rebuilding and reform of the monasteries of England, ruined by earlier Danish invasions and rapine. Edgar made him Archbishop of Canterbury as well as his chief adviser, and for sixteen years Church and State flourished under their wise and disciplined rule. But Fortune's wheel turned against Dunstan once again when Edward, the new king whom he had recently crowned, was murdered by the party of Ethelred the Unready, Edward the Martyr's half-brother. Visionary and outspoken to the last, Dunstan as he crowned Ethelred in 970, boldly foretold the calamities that would attend his unhappy reign, and retired at last from public life. Having seen his prediction all too disastrously fulfilled, eighteen years later he made his last prophecy in a sermon at Canterbury, electrifying the congregation by foretelling his own death on the Feast of the Ascension. He chose his place of burial in the cathedral and died two days later. Even this was Sagittarian, for Sagittarius is the dying and resurrecting sun.

He was not only a talented engineer and metal worker, but an alchemist, if the little book on alchemy which purports to be by him, to be found in the British Library can be trusted. It is a copy dating to the 17th century; whether this treatise (which gives a number of alchemical experiments) is a copy of Dunstan's original or not, it certainly seems likely that his forge was not simply that of a blacksmith as we understand the craft. For the Druid Pheryilt was an order of metal-workers with a secret philosophy, whose craft had metaphysical overtones. Sagittarius is the philisopher's sign. Strange too how bardic Dunstan, his harp slung across his back, echoes our Zodiac's Sagittarius, for the stars of Apollo's Lyre also fall on this effigy's back.

ST BLAISE, c316 AD, is said to have been an Armenian, bishop of Sebaste, who escaped the Roman persecutions of the time by retiring to a cave in the mountains inhabited only by wild beasts. Sensing his saintliness they befriended him and he in turn healed them when they were sick or wounded. Hunters trapping wild beasts for the amphitheatre found him however and took him to Rome, where he was imprisoned and starved in an attempt to make him apostatise. But on the way there he performed two miracles, persuading a wolf who had taken an old woman's pig to restore it to her unharmed, and extracting a fishbone from the throat of a small boy who was choking to death. The old woman, grateful for the return of her pig, saved him from starvation by secretly bringing him food, and moreover provided him with tapers to lighten the Stygian darkness of his cell.

The prison governor then resorted to torture by tearing his flesh with iron combs, and when even this barbarity failed to break his spirit, had him thrown in the sea to drown. But Blaise walked on the water, preaching to the multitude who had gathered to watch him die, and converted many. The governor, desperate by this time, then had him beheaded; a method which proved finally effective.

He is often portrayed with a lighted taper in hand, or holding the seven-toothed comb that tortured him; this last has made him the patron saint of woolcombers, and his day (Feb 3rd) coming next to Candlemas on Feb. 2nd, no doubt accounts for the tale of the tapers smuggled into his gloomy cell. He is still invoked for afflictions of the throat; at St Etheldreda's Ely Place in London they still hold a healing service on his day, placing crossed candles on the throats of sufferers.

In view of this, I hesitate to cast doubt on the very existence of the saint, and if I do, I am only following the devout Butler, who notes in his Lives of the Saints that there seems no evidence for his cult earlier than the 8th century, 400 years or so after he is supposed to have lived. Let no-one in need then be deterred from seeking healing at his service, for there is no doubt about the fact that faith-healing occurs, and that we can attract heavenly powers to aid us by such sympathetic and prayerful ceremonies. Can it be that St Blaise, whoever he may once have been, is one of Jung's archetypes who by traditional reverence has grown in focal power by use like a laser beam, gaining in intensity the more frequently it is reflected back and forth from earth to heaven and back?

Saint Blaise

This said, my main purpose is to speculate on why St Blaise from such faraway and obscure beginnings, became so popular in mediaeval Britain and Europe. I believe that the secret is in his name; that the Church selected him because of it to replace the older festival of Imbolc (one of the four great Celtic fire-festivals of the Druidic year). Imbolc was held early in February to warm flagging spirits at the end of the seemingly endless winter and by sympathetic magic speed the return of the long-absent sun. Similarly, Candlemas was instituted in Rome to replace the pagan festival of Lupercalia. (as Lupus is the latin for wolf, perhaps this accounts for Blaise's obliging predator?)

Blaise like the winter sun retired behind the mountains, surrounded only by the Zodiac animals in his retreat; his dark prison cell lit only by a taper signifying perhaps the sun's faint and feeble February beam. The seven-toothed comb that flayed him was, one suspects, the sun's seven-rayed colour-spectrum; perhaps too the long sunbeams that can sometimes be seen penetrating to earth from breaks in the clouds, like the teeth of a comb.

The sun like St Blaise appears to drown in the sea, and miraculously to rise from this watery death, its path on the waves brilliantly reflected, enlightening (like Blaise) all who see it. He appears with this comb, painted in 1400, on a pillar in Kingston-on-Thames parish church.

His presence here is intriguing, for Kingston seems to be the centre of another terrestrial Zodiac like Glastonbury's; so our sun-saint is once more surrounded by Zodiac animals.

Merlin, we learn from Malory's Morte d'Arthur, had a mysterious master called Blaise who lived in Northumberland. Merlin visited him at *Candlemas* to report on Arthur's battles, for "all the battles that were done in Arthur's days did his master Blaise do write. Also, he did do write all the battles that every worthy knight did of Arthur's court." (Book 1, Chap 15).

The Northumberland hermit's work, if it ever existed, has not survived. Did Malory mean Bede? No, for Bede never mentions Arthur once. There is however an explicit account of Arthur's battles in 9th cent. Nennius which Malory must have read, but Nennius' name can hardly be transmuted into Blaise, and he was a Welshman, not a Northumbrian. Possibly Bleheris, variously spelt Blihis, Bledri – a famous Welsh mastersinger of Arthurian Lays – was in Malory's mind.

Nennius' History of the Britons gives a clue to the nature of Arthur's battles which ties in with Blaise's Zodiacal connections, so is worth considering in this context.

For one thing, there were twelve of them, like the Zodiac signs. For another, at least two of them have been tentatively located on our Zodiac by those who study these matters; the battle on the river Trat Treuroit being assigned to the river Brue (Scorpio, Libra and the Piscean Whale), and the battle on the "mountain" Breguoin being possibly on Cadbury Castle, near Virgo. In another, Arthur bore an image of the Virgin on his shoulders (Virgo again?).

Yet another battle was fought, says Nennius, "at the city of Legion which is called Caer Lion." This is naturally assumed to be Caerleon; but in view of the foregoing sites it is tempting to place it on Leo in our Zodiac.

The last battle, "a most severe contest, when Arthur penetrated to the hill of Badon" is usually ascribed to Bath, as that is the meaning of the name. However, it also means a spring, and there is an equally famous spring at Chalice Well on Glastonbury Tor, the Aquarian Cauldron of Rebirth, and the initiate's final ordeal in these Zodiac Mysteries. One is reminded of Kentigern's final bath, and that of Llew the sun-god in the Mabinogion, which he took with one foot on the Capricornian goat's back, the other on the Piscean river bank, flying upward as an eagle in death. It seems he was in Aquarius, which in Druidic times was the winter solstice, the sun's weakest hour.

I am not the first to wonder whether these battles are not in fact garbled memories of the initiate Arthur's progress (like the Twelve Labours of Hercules) through the Zodiac Mysteries.

Malory's next passage gives substance to this theory. The day after his visit to Blaise at Candlemas Merlin returns to Arthur, disguised as a hunter and armed with a bow and arrows to demand a gift in return for a secret. Arthur fails to recognise his magician and rather snobbishly demands to know why he should give to a churl. "Sir", said Merlin, "ye were better to give me a gift than to lose great riches; for here, in the same place where the great battle was, is great treasure hid in the earth". I hope I may be forgiven for interpreting this secret treasure as the Terrestrial Zodiac. I suspect too that Merlin, as an archer dressed in thick furs, was impersonating Arthur as wintry Sagittarius, as a subtle means of telling him that he did not "know himself", and was even unaware that he was in the Mysteries, or that his actions would be judged in that light. (A state that is shared by most of us, most of the time). For nothing more is said of the treasure, or any attempt on Arthur's part to find it, or even show an interest in the subject.

Significantly, Malory then launches into an exposé of Arthur's misdeeds; he has a passing fancy for the beautiful Lionors and begets a son upon her; the next minute he meets and falls for Guinevere at her father Leodegrance's castle, but before he marries her has another affair with Morgause (unbeknown to him his own half-sister, and already married to King Lot of the Orkneys), the child of this brief union being the desperate Mordred, his final undoing. "The gods are just, and of our pleasant vices make instruments to plague us."

It is surely no accident that Leodegrance stands for Leo, the first of Hercules' Twelve labours being the Nemean Lion. Is Malory not indicating that Arthur has failed his first trial, that of Leo's House of Love?

And is it coincidence merely that Merlin, last of the sun-worshipping Druids, had for tutor a master with such a luminous name? Merlin, we are told, made the Round Table, which is the Zodiac, the sun's path through the sky. I suspect that both Master and pupil fashioned it together, "for the salvation of men."

INDEX

Adonis-Eshmun, 70
Amalech, 16
Ambrosius Aurelianus, 22
Anahita, 16
Anna, 9, 16, 25, 49, 66
Annunciation, 5, 7, 63
Apple of Discord, 136
Arthur, 6, 11-16, 21-23, 28, 34, 36-40, 44, 53, 56-57, 61, 64-65, 69, 71, 74-75, 78-81, 83, 85, 88-90, 92, 95-96, 102-103, 105-107, 115-120, 123, 125, 127-128, 135, 147-148
Asser, 8, 23, 119
Awen, 7, 55, 93, 95-96, 111-112

Baal, 8, 16
Bladud, 136
Bride's Corn Dolly, 5
Brigantia, 5, 46, 49-50, 109
Britannia, 9, 49

Cairnech, 58
Candlemas, 145-148
Caradoc, 31-34, 106-107
Cathars, 30, 104
Cathars, 30, 104
Cauldron of Ceridwen, 46, 51
Cei, 88, 120
Ceredwen Ogiervran Amhad, 132
Cernunnos, 5, 127
Chalice Well, 24-25, 37, 44, 123, 147
Conan Meriadoc, 136
Cunobelinus, 8, 32

Dionysus, 73, 106-107
Draco, 2, 13, 15, 58, 70, 102, 131
Druidic Order of the Pheryllt, 58

Ector, 13-14, 117
Edeyrn ap Nudd, 127
Eurgen, 31-34

Galahad, 13-15, 24, 40, 103, 112, 125
Gawain, 12-14, 69, 75, 95, 102-103
Gemini, Messianic Effigy, 5
Gemini's Three Bars of Light, 5
Gildas, 19-21, 44, 54, 59, 62, 82-83, 106-107, 114, 124-126
Girt Dog of Langport, 2, 129
Glastonbury Abbey, 5, 12, 27, 34, 74, 78, 140
Glastonbury Tor, 5-6, 63, 26, 147
Gnostic Gospel of Bartho mew, 64
Gorlassar, 119
Guinevere, 11, 13-14, 38, 78 9, 85, 103, 115-116, 135, 148
Gwyn ap Nudd, 28-29, 37, 12 129

Herne, 127-128

Inis Wytryn, 82
John of Glastonbury, 28, 44
Joseph of Arimathea, 4-5, 15, 24, 26, 29, 31, 33-34, 39, 52, 57, 60, 64, 84, 91, 123

Kai, 95-96, 116

Lancelot, 12-15, 24, 38, 78
Le Matiere de Bretagne, 12
Leodegrance, 14, 135, 148
Little St Hugh, 4, 98
Logres, 13-14, 16, 89, 96, 102-103
Lupercalia, 146

Mabon, 18, 42, 70, 83, 88-97
Magnus Clemens Maximus, 22, 137
Melkin, 4, 28, 34, 64
Melkin's Prophecy, 4, 28
Mordred, 13-15, 81, 107, 115, 148

Neith, 37, 126
Nicor, 95
Nodens, 37, 126

150

Pelles, 12-13, 15
Percival, 14
Perlesvaus, 12-14, 16, 30, 36, 95
Phoenicians, 8-9, 29, 34, 66, 70
Prince Macsen, 22, 66, 136

Robert de Borron, 34-36
Rufus Pudens, 32-33

Scorpio, 2, 5, 13-14, 69, 141, 143, 147
Ship of Fools, 140
Skiffs of St Ursula, 138, 140
Solomon's Ship, 14, 25, 40, 112
St Beon, 4, 43
St Blaise, 5, 145-146
St Brigit, 4, 44-45, 73
St Budoc, 4, 73-74, 98
St Cadoc, 5, 66, 85, 120-123, 126, 131
St Cadvan, 4, 65, 87
St Carantoc, 4, 56, 59-60, 66, 69
St Clement, 5, 84, 111-112
St Collen, 4, 37, 39-40, 74
St David, 4, 51-57, 66, 70, 74, 82, 96,
    130, 139
St Decuman, 4, 74
St Dunstan, 5, 39, 140
St Edeyrn, 5, 126-129
St Edeyrn, 5, 126-129
St Eval, 4, 83-84, 115
St Ffili, 4, 82
St Gengulf or Winwaloe, 4, 97
St Germanus, 5, 41, 117, 126
St Gwodloew, 105
St Gwynnlyw & St Tathan, 5, 120-121
St Helier, 5, 110-111
St Huail, 5, 106
St Hywel, 5, 107
St Ilid, 4, 31
St Issui, 4, 85
St Kea Colodoc, 5, 114
St Kenelm's Tympanun, 5
St Kenelm, 5, 108-110
St Keneth, 4, 80-82, 109, 111, 115, 117-
    118
St Kentigern or Mungo, 4, 75

St Keyne, 5, 18, 75, 85, 87, 130-132
St Mabyn, 4, 73, 83, 87, 89
St Madron, 4, 97
St Maternus, 4, 97
St Melor, 4, 16, 77-78, 102
St Nunn, 4, 51, 55, 96
St Padarn, 4, 52-53, 64
St Patrick, 4, 41-45, 47, 51, 58, 82, 100,
    111, 125
St Petroc, 4, 66, 71
St Rioche, 4, 101
St Roch, 5, 102
St Roche of Montpellier, 5, 103
St Sulien, 4, 87
St Ursula, 5, 136, 138, 140
StWillow, 5

Tacitus, 32, 34, 138
Templars, 62, 64, 104
The 3 Eves of Evesham, 5
The Doorty Cross, 5, 17
The God Esus, 5, 86
The Grail-stone of Parzival, 4, 60
The Holy Boy, 4, 73, 111
The Triple Goddess, 5, 134-136
Tree-Alphabet, 110
Tristram, 13-15, 38, 79, 114

Vortigern, 22, 109, 118-119, 126

Wearyall Hill, 12, 15, 24, 70

Other books of interest from Capall Bann:

Angels & Goddesses - Celtic Christianity & Paganism in Ancient Britain
By Michael Howard

Traces the history & development of Celtic Paganism & Christianity specifically in Wales, but also in relation to the rest of the British Isles including Ireland, from the Iron Age to the present. A study of the transition between the pagan religions & Christianity & how the early Church, in the Celtic countries struggled with & later absorbed the earlier forms of spirituality, clearly seen in the development of Celtic Christianity when pagan & Christian beliefs co-existed, albeit in an uneasy & sometimes violent relationship. Also covers how the Roman Catholic version of Christianity arrived in England at the end of the 6th century & its affect on the Celtic Church; how Celtic Christianity was suppressed & the effect this was to have on the history & theology of the Church in the Middle Ages. The influence of Celtic Christianity on the Arthurian legends & the Grail romances is explored, as is the resurgence of interest in Celtic Christianity today.

ISBN 1898307 032   £9.95   169 pages

Kecks, Keddles and Kesh by Michael Bayley
Celtic Language Survival, Lovespoons and the Cog Almanac

The cog almanac is a traditional permanent calendar, carved in wood which used regular meteor showers to tell the time of year and specific festival dates, both those of the Christian church and of festivals stretching far back in history. Based on oral family traditions, Michael Bayley argues the survival of the Celtic language in central England and discusses the secret language of English lovespoons. For those with eyes to see and ears to hear, a fascinating wealth of the Old Knowledge reveals itself here.

ISBN 1898307 628   £11.95   Profusely Illustrated

Caer Sidhe - The Celtic Night Sky Vol 1 by Michael Bayley

The Celtic tribes of ancient Europe saw nearly the same night sky as we do, except that it was clearer. The constellations were the same, but they were interpreted in a different way, with different names and interpretations. Caer Sidhe explores the Celtic night sky maps, the constellations of the zodiac and the moving stars, the associated deities and legends, uses of dene holes (as used by Merlin to view the stars) and much, much more fascinating information. Profusely illustrated with maps and drawings.

ISBN 1 86163 014X £10.95R97   Profusely Illustrated

The Circle and the Square by Jack Gale

Past-life memories and proven questing techniques combine in this original, amazing and provocative study of the occult background to the Tor executions of the Glastonbury Three in 1539. Using psychically received material with archival research, Jack Gale takes the reader through the strange magical and alchemical underworld of early Tudor Glastonbury. Here, guardian thought-forms who watch over hidden sacred treasures and secret ritual marriages, still dimly reflected in the imagery of the great landscape zodiac, conceive awesome, living energies. The Avalonian earth and its mysteries are viewed from a radically fresh perspective, raising many profound questions in the reader's mind.

ISBN 186163 013 1   £10.95

FREE DETAILED CATALOGUE

A detailed illustrated catalogue is available on request, SAE or International Postal Coupon appreciated. Titles are available direct from Capall Bann, post free in the UK (cheque or PO with order) or from good bookshops and specialist outlets. Titles currently available include:

Angels and Goddesses - Celtic Christianity & Paganism by Michael Howard
Arthur - The Legend Unveiled by C Johnson & E Lung
Auguries and Omens - The Magical Lore of Birds by Yvonne Aburrow
Book of the Veil The by Peter Paddon
Caer Sidhe - Celtic Astrology and Astronomy by Michael Bayley
Call of the Horned Piper by Nigel Jackson
Cats' Company by Ann Walker
Celtic Faery Shamanism by Catrin James
Celtic Sacifice - Pre Christian Ritual & Religion by Marion Pearce
Celtic Lore & Druidic Ritual by Rhiannon Ryall
Crystal Clear - A Guide to Quartz Crystal by Jennifer Dent
Earth Dance - A Year of Pagan Rituals by Jan Brodie
Earth Harmony - Places of Power, Holiness and Healing by Nigel Pennick
Earth Magic by Margaret McArthur
Enchanted Forest - The Magical Lore of Trees by Yvonne Aburrow
Familiars - Animal Powers of Britain by Anna Franklin
Healing Homes by Jennifer Dent
Herbcraft - Shamanic & Ritual Use of Herbs by Susan Lavender & Anna Franklin
In Search of Herne the Hunter by Eric Fitch
Inner Space Workbook - Developing Counselling & Magical Skills Through the Tarot
Magical Incenses and Perfumes by Jan Brodie
Magical Lore of Cats by Marion Davies
Magical Lore of Herbs by Marion Davies
Masks of Misrule - The Horned God & His Cult in Europe by Nigel Jackson
Mysteries of the Runes by Michael Howard
Oracle of Geomancy by Nigel Pennick
Patchwork of Magic by Julia Day
Pathworking - A Practical Book of Guided Meditations by Pete Jennings
Pickingill Papers - The Origins of Gardnerian Wicca by Michael Howard
Practical Spirituality by Steve Hounsome
Psychic Animals by Dennis Bardens
Psychic Self Defence - Real Solutions by Jan Brodie
Runic Astrology by Nigel Pennick
Sacred Animals by Gordon MacLellan
Sacred Grove - The Mysteries of the Forest by Yvonne Aburrow
Sacred Geometry by Nigel Pennick
Sacred Lore of Horses The by Marion Davies
Sacred Ring - Pagan Origins British Folk Festivals & Customs by Michael Howard
Seasonal Magic - Diary of a Village Witch by Paddy Slade
Secret Places of the Goddess by Philip Heselton
Talking to the Earth by Gordon Maclellan
The Goddess Year by Nigel Pennick & Helen Field
West Country Wicca by Rhiannon Ryall

Capall Bann is owned and run by people actively involved in many of the areas in which we publish. Our list is expanding rapidly so do contact us for details on the latest releases.

Capall Bann Publishing, Freshfields, Chieveley, Berks, RG20 8TF